G. Frederick Wright

The Divine Authority of the Bible

G. Frederick Wright

The Divine Authority of the Bible

ISBN/EAN: 9783337780203

Printed in Europe, USA, Canada, Australia, Japan

Cover: Foto ©Lupo / pixelio.de

More available books at **www.hansebooks.com**

THE
DIVINE AUTHORITY

OF

THE BIBLE.

BY

G. FREDERICK WRIGHT,

PROFESSOR OF THE LANGUAGE AND LITERATURE OF THE NEW
TESTAMENT IN OBERLIN THEOLOGICAL SEMINARY; AUTHOR
OF "THE LOGIC OF CHRISTIAN EVIDENCES," "STUDIES
IN SCIENCE AND RELIGION," "RELATION OF
DEATH TO PROBATION," ETC., ETC.

BOSTON:

Congregational Sunday-School and Publishing Society,

CONGREGATIONAL HOUSE.

TO

The Memory of my Sainted Parents,

WALTER AND MARY PEABODY WRIGHT,

WHOSE WISDOM IN CHOOSING THE BIBLE FOR THE RELIGIOUS
GUIDE OF THEIR FAMILY HAS BEEN VERIFIED BY
ALL THE EXPERIENCE AND STUDY OF
THEIR GRATEFUL SON,

THIS BOOK IS DEDICATED

BY THE AUTHOR.

PREFACE.

The present brief treatise is an outgrowth of special studies in inductive logic, begun in the midst of pastoral labors sixteen or seventeen years ago; and considerable portions of it were written at that time. The author found himself, as nearly all young pastors do when coming in practical contact with the unbelief of the age, compelled as never before to give a reason for the faith that was in him; and was continually called upon to answer in the presence of the doubtful and unbelieving such questions as these: 1. What are both the general and specific grounds of confidence in the truths of the Christian religion? The author's answer to this question may be found in the little treatise on "The Logic of Christian Evidences," published four years ago. 2. How can the infalli-

tant from that which is irrelevant to the discussion, the volume is offered to all candid seekers after the truth upon the momentous questions involved.

G. FREDERICK WRIGHT.

OBERLIN, OHIO, June 2, 1884.

TABLE OF CONTENTS.

[Subjects are referred to by paragraphs; Chapters by pages.]

CHAPTER I.

INTRODUCTION.

The Question one of Interpretation — Sphere of Inspiration, 1; Logic as well as Learning necessary, 2; Christianity essentially Supernatural, 3-5; Therefore Inspiration probable, 6. (pp. 13-17.)

CHAPTER II.

THE PROMISE OF INSPIRATION.

Unique Position of the Primitive Church, 7; The Apostolic Commission, 8, 9; Miraculous Power exercised, 10-13; Appealed to, 14. (pp. 18-25.)

CHAPTER III.

THE DIVINE AUTHORITY OF THE BIBLE CLAIMED AND ASSERTED.

The Council at Jerusalem, 15; Claims of Paul, 16, 17; Peter's Acknowledgment of Paul, 18; Paul's Disclaimers considered, 19, 20; The Book of Revelation, 21; All Inspired Scripture profitable, 22; The New Testament endorses the Old, 23, 24; The Scripture a Definite Collection of Books, 25; Objections considered, 26; The Scriptures a Unit, 27; Subdivisions of Scripture, 28; Singular that Christ quoted nothing but the Old Testament, 29; Theory of Accommodation inadmissible, 30; Old Testament Writers claimed Inspiration, — Summary of Argument, 31. (pp. 26-54.)

CHAPTER IV.

THE CANON OF THE OLD TESTAMENT.

Canon defined, 32; What constituted the Scriptures to which Christ appealed? 33; Testimony of Jesus, the Son of Sirach, 34; Of the Apocrypha in general, 35; Josephus, 36; Philo Judæus, 37; Melito, Bishop of Sardis, and Origen, 38; Jerome and the Talmud, 39; Canonicity of the Apocrypha unsustained, 40; Reasons for its Adoption by the Romish Church, 41. (pp. 55-68.)

CHAPTER V.

THE CANON OF THE NEW TESTAMENT.

Never formally settled, but Practical Unanimity reached before the Close of the Fourth Century by Common Consent, 42; Testimony of the Second Century, 43; Inherent Weight of this Testimony, 44; Evidence in Detail, 45; For the Epistle to the Hebrews, 46; Epistle of Jude, 47; James, 48; Second and Third John, 49; Second Peter, 50; The Revelation of John, 51; Superiority of the New Testament to the Epistle of Barnabas, 52; The Shepherd of Hermas, 53; The New Testament all written or endorsed by Apostles, 54. (pp. 69-84.)

CHAPTER VI.

INSPIRATION AND TEXTUAL CRITICISM.

Inspiration belongs only to the Autographs, 56; Material from which to determine the True Text, 57; Small Margin of Uncertainty, 58; Character of the Mass of Textual Variations, 59; Textual Criticism confirms rather than unsettles Confidence, 60; Some of the Important Passages affected by Textual Criticism, 61; The Sinaitic and the Vatican Manuscripts proved to be the Best as well as the Oldest, 62; Natural Origin of Variations in the Text, 63, 64; Textual Criticism a Science, 65. (pp. 85-100.)

CHAPTER VII.

INTERPRETATION OF SCRIPTURE.

Fallible Interpreters of an Infallible Record, 66; Necessity of Reverence, 67; A Perfect Revelation must be in Human

CONTENTS. xi

Form, 68; The Obscure should be explained by what is more Clear, 69, 70; Interpret Scripture by Scripture, 71; Did the Writers of the New Testament know how to interpret the Old — Professors Toy and Ladd, Criticised, 72; Christ a Good Interpreter, 73; Christ's Interpretation of the Old Testament, 74; Paul's, 75; Formulas of Quotation, 76; Difficult Quotations in Hebrews, 77; Pregnant Language, 78; Did Christ and Paul teach a Speedy Second Coming? 79; True Conservatism, 80; Things preliminary to Interpretation, 81; Elasticity of Language, 82; Illustrated in explaining the Alleged Discrepancy regarding the Time of the Last Passover, 83; Still Language conveys Thought, 84; Formula for Interpretation, 85; Definite Results possible, 86; The Bible intelligible, 87. (pp. 101-150.)

CHAPTER VIII.

SUMMARY OF POSITIVE ARGUMENT.

There are Difficulties, 88; Argument condensed, 89; Tradition of the Second Century all-important, 90; Intrinsic Excellence of the New Testament, 91; Testimony ample, 92; Burden of Proof, 93. (pp. 151-156.)

CHAPTER IX.

INHERENT DIFFICULTIES OF THE SUBJECT.

Mode of Inspiration not essential, 94; Analogy with Nature, 95; God's Designs many-sided, 96; Practical Character of the Discussion, 97; Analogy with the Doctrine of Christ's Nature, 98, 99; Elasticity of Language again, 100; True Accommodation, 101, 102; Reality of Demoniacal Possession, 103; Error belongs to Interpreters rather than to the Bible, 104. (pp. 157-170.)

CHAPTER X.

ALLEGED VERBAL DISCREPANCIES OF THE BIBLE.

Numerous in the Gospels, 105; Healing of Peter's Wife's Mother, 106; Christ stilling the Tempest, 107; Christ and the Rich Young Man, 108; Christ and the Pharisees on Divorce, 109; Diverse Inscriptions on the Cross, 110; Instructions given to the Twelve, 111, 112; Sermon on the Mount, 113, 114; There is Little that is New on the Subject, 115. (pp. 171-183.)

CHAPTER XI.

ALLEGED ERRORS OF THE NEW TESTAMENT IN QUOTING THE OLD.

Christ's Reference to the Flood, 116; to the Famine in the Time of Elijah, 117; Quotation of Isa. xxix. 13, 118; Quotations in the Book of Hebrews, 119, 120; Summary of Results, 121. (pp. 184-194.)

CHAPTER XII.

HARMONY OF THE BIBLE WITH SCIENCE.

Genesis and Geology — First Theory of Reconciliation, 122; Second Theory, 123; Either Theory confirms the Bible, 124; Chronology of the Bible, 125; Chronology of Science, 126. (pp. 195-203.)

CHAPTER XIII.

PORTIONS OF SCRIPTURE SAID TO BE INSIGNIFICANT OR UNWORTHY OF INSPIRATION.

Analogies between Nature and the Bible, 127; Inspiration, like Design in Nature, Comprehensive, 128; Comprehensiveness of the Design of the Bible, 129; Alleged Literary Infelicities, 130; The Bible an Organic Whole, 131; The Naturalness of the Bible a Part of its Perfection, 132; The Bible adapted to all Ages and Classes, 133; The Sterner Characteristics of the Bible still useful, 134; The Genealogical Tables still valuable, 135. (pp. 204-217.)

CHAPTER XIV.

GENERAL SUMMARY.

The Argument inductive — Method of Agreement, 136; Method of Difference, 137; Unity in Diversity of the Bible, 138; Its Freedom from Error, 139; The Harmony Profound, 140; The Writers avoid Speculation, 141; The Cause must be Divine, 142; Self-possession of the Writers, 143; Providential Preservation of the Writers, 144; Accuracy of the Known gives Confidence to the Whole Testimony, 145; We can believe the Bible where not confirmed by other Evidence, 146; The Word of God sure, 147. (pp. 218-232.)

THE
DIVINE AUTHORITY OF THE BIBLE.

I.

INTRODUCTION.

1. ADMITTING that the more important books of the New Testament were written in apostolic times, and were generally accepted as authentic by the Christians of the first and second centuries,[1] the question concerning the divine authority of these writings is largely one of interpretation. The question of the divine authority of the Old Testament likewise depends in large measure upon our interpretation of the words of Christ and his apostles as recorded in the New Testament.

In treating of the divine authority of the Bible, we cannot well avoid using the word inspiration, but we would define the word with reference to the results attained rather than with reference to the divine process through which the results have been secured. In calling the Scriptures inspired

---

[1] The general question as to the credibility of the New Testament has been discussed by the author in a preceding treatise, the Logic of Christian Evidences. Andover: W. F. Draper. 1880.

and infallible, we intend to say that they are an adequate and authoritative record of the divine revelation upon which the Christian religion is founded, and that therefore they are, when properly interpreted, the final appeal in all distinctive questions of Christian faith and practice. For reasons which will appear as the discussion proceeds, we prefer to retain the ordinary evangelical terms, and say, "the Bible *is* the word of God" and "the Bible *is* a revelation of God," rather than the more ambiguous phrases, "the Bible *contains* the word of God" and "the Bible *contains* a revelation." But the use of these terms does not shut us off from considering: 1st. What books constitute the Bible? 2d. What corruptions are to be eliminated from the text? 3d. What meaning was the language of the Bible designed to convey? Language is a means, and not an end. It is the sense and not the sound of scriptural language which has authority.

2. Our decision with reference to the authority of Sacred Scripture is not dependent solely upon the extent of our learning, but largely upon the soundness of our judgment in estimating the weight of the well-established facts which are most central in the argument. Logic is even more important than learning in determining the extent of the authority with which the Sacred Scriptures invest themselves. It is our business as investigators to

adhere to those facts which are fullest, clearest, and most fundamental in their bearing upon the question. If these facts seem to shut us off from the vague fields of speculation, in which our minds could rove unfettered, we are bound to remember that in all inductive researches *fancy* is compelled thus to wait on *fact*.

3. Before attending directly to the specific facts bearing on the question concerning the divine origin of the Scriptures of the Old and New Testaments, it is important to consider the degree to which the supernatural element pervades the Christian religion. This supernatural element in Jewish history and in Christianity is alike surprising for its extent and for its limitations. A miraculous dispensation begins with Abraham and ends with the apostles, — with an intermission of about four hundred years between Malachi and John the Baptist. All the books of the Bible received as canonical by Protestants are, as we shall show in the proper place, supposed on good grounds to have been written during these two periods of special miraculous intervention. Outside of these books there is no trustworthy account of any special divine revelation. An important part of our inquiry therefore relates to the adequacy of this revelation and of its record in the Bible.

4. The acknowledged supernatural character of Christianity has an important bearing upon every

department both of Christian evidences and of biblical interpretation. We are never at liberty to forget that the distinctive facts of Christianity are miraculous, and that its characteristic doctrines depend for authority on supernatural endorsement. The corner-stone of our faith is the resurrection of Christ. Christ died and was buried, but on the third day he arose from the dead, and in due time ascended to heaven in the presence of his disciples. He who accepts this stupendous miracle will find little difficulty in crediting the minor miracles recorded in the Gospels. The scientific caution which can be carried by the force of evidence over the miracle of the resurrection — which lies at the threshold of Christianity — will find few additional impediments in the remaining miracles of the New Testament.

5. A proper appreciation of the supernatural character of Christianity likewise removes the antecedent improbability which would otherwise attach itself to the miracles of the Old Testament. The two dispensations stand or fall together, and the evidence in favor of each is confirmatory of both. In accepting the crowning miracle of Christianity we acknowledge the presence of a cause which is fully adequate to the production of all the other alleged supernatural facts of Sacred Scripture, and at the same time concede the existence of a reason or final cause sufficiently important

to remove all supposed antecedent probability against the introduction of miracles.

6. The miraculous facts of Christianity also prepare the way for our belief in (and indeed make antecedently probable) the exercise of a supernatural agency sufficient to secure such an authoritative, intelligible, and adequate written record and exposition of the facts and doctrines of the gospel as is essential to its continued preservation and propagation in the world. It is scarcely credible that such a stupendous system of supernatural agencies as was deemed necessary to introduce Christianity, should be left without an intelligible, authoritative, and adequate record. Still, the difficulty of determining beforehand, upon general principles, what the Creator ought to do, is so great that we should not rely too much upon this class of evidence in ascertaining what he has actually done. It is more important to turn first to the Bible itself, in whose general credibility we already believe, to learn what the sacred writers themselves say of the authority by which they speak, and to ascertain from direct examination the various literary and other characteristics of the volume; and secondly, to the history of the primitive church, to ascertain the value set upon the books of the Old and New Testaments by those who, by reason of proximity both in time and place, were most competent to estimate the validity of their claims.

II.

THE PROMISE OF INSPIRATION.

7. THE primitive church was unique in its relation to the founder of Christianity. The first believers enjoyed the presence and the personal instruction of their Lord. They declared that which they had heard, that which they had seen with their eyes and beheld, and their hands had handled, concerning the Word of life.[1] The apostles and their companions can therefore, on this account, speak with a degree of authority which no other writers could claim. But, besides this superior advantage of position with reference to their Master, the authority of the apostles is enhanced by various remarkable and definite promises given them both when they were chosen and at a later period of their Lord's ministry.

8. When the apostles were set apart, Jesus intimated to them that they were to be delivered up to judgment before synagogues, and rulers, and authorities; but he warned them not to be anxious concerning their answer and defence; for he

---

[1] 1 John i. 1.

THE PROMISE OF INSPIRATION.   19

assured them, "the Holy Spirit shall teach you in that very hour what ye ought to say." "It is not ye that speak, but the Spirit of your Father that speaketh in you."[1] Our estimate of the supernatural character of this promise is augmented by the fact that Christ bestowed upon these disciples the power of performing miracles. And he "gave them authority over unclean spirits, to cast them out, and to heal all manner of disease and all manner of sickness."[2]

9. The fourteenth, fifteenth, and sixteenth chapters of John describe the scene when Jesus discoursed with the apostles for the last time before his crucifixion. Upon this solemn occasion he repeated to them, with added emphasis and illustration, the promises given upon their induction into the apostolic office. He assures them that the Father will send in his own name the Comforter, even the Holy Spirit, who shall teach them all things, and bring to their remembrance all that he has said unto them.[3] That this promise is specially applicable to the apostles and their companions, and is limited to them, is indicated in the fact that the Spirit was to quicken their memory so that they could *recall* the verbal teachings of Christ. A similar promise is given in the following chapter, where the Comforter, "even the

[1] Matt. x. 19. 20; Mark xiii. 11; Luke xii. 11, 12; cf. also Luke xxi. 14, 15.
[2] Matt. x. 1; Luke ix. 1.   [3] John xiv. 26.

Spirit of truth which proceedeth from the Father," is again promised to his disciples, and Christ assures them that the Comforter "shall bear witness of me: and ye also bear witness, because ye have been with me from the beginning."[1] Again, the Saviour tells the apostles that " when he, the Spirit of truth, is come, he shall guide you into all the truth, . . . and he shall declare unto you the things that are to come. He shall glorify me; for he shall take of mine, and shall declare it unto you."[2] Such was the commission of the apostles; and so precise and emphatic was the authority with which they were invested to speak in Christ's name. Is it possible to believe that the Spirit would be given to secure accuracy in the *spoken* word, and not also be given to secure perfection in the *written* word? No. For the principle is certainly valid, that the Lord who promises to provide for the less important emergency, will take even greater care to provide for the more important want. The promise is therefore comprehensive, and includes the written word as well as the spoken.

10. We have abundant evidence that the part of Christ's promise to the apostles relating to their power to perform miracles, was literally fulfilled. When the seventy returned from their journey, it was "with joy, saying, Lord, even the devils are subject unto us in thy name."[3] After

---
[1] John xv. 26, 27.   [2] John xvi. 12-15.   [3] Luke x. 17.

Christ's ascension, we read in the Acts of a great variety of miracles performed by the apostles and their associates. In connection with the outpouring of the Spirit, at the day of Pentecost, we are told that "many wonders and signs were done by the apostles";[1] and it was not much later that Peter and John publicly, in the name of Jesus Christ of Nazareth, healed by a word a lame man who had been a cripple from birth.[2] The death of Ananias and Sapphira must also be regarded as miraculous.[3] And it is added in immediate connection that (12) "by the hands of the apostles were many signs and wonders wrought among the people; and they were all with one accord in Solomon's porch. (13) But of the rest durst no man join himself to them; howbeit the people magnified them; (14) and believers were the more added to the Lord, multitudes both of men and women; (15) insomuch that they even carried out the sick into the streets, and laid them on beds and couches, that, as Peter came by, at the least his shadow might overshadow some one of them. (16) And there also came together the multitude from the cities round about Jerusalem, bringing sick folk, and them that were vexed with unclean spirits; and they were healed every one."[4]

At a later period we read that when Peter went

---

[1] Acts ii. 43.   [2] Acts iii. 1–10.
[3] Acts v. 1–11.   [4] Acts v. 12–16.

down to Lydda he found there (33) "a certain man named Æneas, which had kept his bed eight years; for he was palsied. (34) And Peter said unto him, Æneas, Jesus Christ healeth thee: arise, and make thy bed. And straightway he arose. (35) And all that dwelt at Lydda and in Sharon saw him, and they turned to the Lord."[1]

At the same time, near by, at Joppa, Peter is reported to have restored Dorcas unto life.[2] In connection with both these miracles we are informed that many believed on the Lord."[3]

11. Stephen, also, obtained his remarkable influence not only because he was full of grace and power, but also because he "wrought great wonders and signs among the people."[4]

12. Philip, likewise, is reported to have publicly exercised miraculous power, both to convince the people of Samaria and to confound a celebrated sorcerer of that city named Simon. (5) "And Philip went down to the city of Samaria, and proclaimed unto them the Christ. (6) And the multitudes gave heed with one accord unto the things that were spoken by Philip, when they heard and saw the signs which he did. (7) For *from* many of those which had unclean spirits, they came out, crying with a loud voice: and many that were palsied, and that were lame, were healed. (8) And there was

---

[1] Acts ix. 33–35.   [2] Acts ix. 36–41.
[3] Acts ix. 42.   [4] Acts vi. 8.

much joy in that city. . . . (13)And Simon also himself believed : and being baptized, he continued with Philip ; and beholding signs and great miracles wrought, he was amazed."¹

13. The miracles ascribed to Paul are as numerous as those to Peter. On their first missionary journey Paul and Barnabas, while on the island of Cyprus, were opposed by Elymas, the sorcerer. Paul was enabled to resist him by bringing upon him a miraculous blindness. " And now, behold, the hand of the Lord is upon thee, and thou shalt be blind, not seeing the sun for a season. And immediately there fell on him a mist and a darkness ; and he went about seeking some to lead him by the hand."² On the same journey, at Iconium, we are told that when Paul and Barnabas spoke boldly in the Lord, the Lord bore " witness unto the word of his grace, granting signs and wonders to be done by their hands."³ And at Lystra Paul is related to have publicly healed a man who had been a helpless cripple from his birth.⁴

On the second missionary journey, when Paul reached Philippi, he was annoyed by a young woman said to have been possessed with a spirit of divination. And "Paul, being sore troubled, turned and said to the spirit, I charge thee in the

---

¹ Acts viii. 5-8, 13. ² Acts xiii. 11.
³ Acts xiv. 3. ⁴ Acts xiv. 10.

name of Jesus Christ to come out of her. And it came out that very hour."¹

Upon his third missionary journey, it is related that while Paul was preaching at Troas a certain young man, named Eutychus, fell from a third story window, " and was taken up dead. ⁽¹⁰⁾ And Paul went down, and fell on him, and embracing him said, Make ye no ado; for his life is in him. . . . ⁽¹²⁾ And they brought the lad alive, and were not a little comforted."²

Again, during the voyage to Rome the barbarous inhabitants of Melita saw Paul bitten by a viper without suffering harm, and were persuaded that he was a god.³ At the same time, also, Paul prayed, and laid his hands upon the father of Publius, and thereby healed him of the fever and dysentery with which he was prostrated. "And when this was done, the rest also which had diseases in the island came, and were cured."⁴

14. With this enumeration of apostolic miracles should be connected a passage in Hebrews, where the writer confidently appeals, as if it were well known to his readers, to the fact that the great salvation, which was at first ⁽³⁾ "spoken through the Lord, was confirmed unto us by them that heard; ⁽⁴⁾ God also bearing witness with them, both by signs and wonders, and by manifold powers, and

¹ Acts xvi. 18. ² Acts xx. 10, 12.
³ Acts xxviii. 1-6. ⁴ Acts xxviii. 9.

by gifts of the Holy Ghost, according to his own will:"[1] Paul makes a similar appeal in his letter to the church at Rome, affirming that to secure the obedience of the Gentiles, Christ worked through him " by word and deed, in the power of signs and wonders, in the power of the Holy Ghost."[2] In the Second Epistle to the Corinthians Paul makes a like appeal to well-known miracles by which his apostolic authority had been established before them. [11] "For in nothing was I behind the very chiefest apostles, though I am nothing. [12] Truly the signs of an apostle were wrought among you in all patience, by signs and wonders and mighty works."[3]

It thus appears that the apostles and their companions were led by Christ to expect supernatural confirmation of the truth they were commissioned to preach; and that, according to the whole history, such confirmation was abundantly provided. This fact greatly increases the antecedent presumption that supernatural aid would be granted to secure for coming ages an authentic and authoritative record of the original facts and doctrines out of which Christianity as a living force has sprung, and upon which it must ever depend for its characteristic motives to activity.

[1] Heb. ii. 3, 4.   [2] Rom. xv. 18, 19.   [3] 2 Cor. xii. 11, 12.

III.

THE DIVINE AUTHORITY OF THE BIBLE CLAIMED AND ASSERTED.

15. WE will next examine the writings of the New Testament, to ascertain whether the apostles claimed the fulfilment in themselves of the promises of the special presence with them of the Holy Spirit. Turning to Acts xv. 28, we find the disciples closing the deliberations of a most important council with the following remarkable words: "For it seemed good to the Holy Ghost, and to us, to lay upon you no greater burden than these necessary things." It would seem difficult to devise a more distinct statement of the actual possession of a divine commission, and of divine authority, than is found in the clause here, which identifies as one the judgment of the Holy Ghost and that of the apostles.

16. In the writings of Paul the claim of divine authority for his words is most frequently put forth. The comparative silence of the other apostles as to their authority, doubtless arises from the fact that there was no class of believers who ever disputed it. The authority of Paul, however, was

repeatedly challenged, and his right to be classed among the apostles had to be established in face of the fact that he had not been a companion of the Lord, but had communed with him only in visions and trances. It is well, therefore, to notice how emphatically and repeatedly he claims the authority of apostleship, — a claim which in his lifetime became universally recognized. In the earliest of his Epistles[1] we find him thanking God that when the church at Thessalonica received the word of the message, even the word of God from him, they "accepted *it* not *as* the word of men, but, as it is in truth, the word of God." In other Epistles of this same period, the claim of divine authority for his own words is often repeated. He distinctly asserts his apostleship in as many as nine Epistles. In the first verse of Romans, he declares he was "called *to be* an apostle," and later in the Epistle he styles himself the "apostle of the Gentiles."[2] And he congratulates the church at Ephesus, that they are "built upon the foundation of the apostles and prophets, Christ Jesus himself being the chief corner-stone."[3] The confidence with which the primitive Christians regarded the facts upon which their hopes of salvation rested, appears in a strik-

---

[1] 1 Thess. ii. 13.
[2] See similar assertions 1 Cor. i. 1; ix. 1, 2; xv. 9; 2 Cor. i. 1; xi. 5; xii. 11, 12; Gal. i. 1; Eph. i. 1; Col. i. 1; 1 Tim. i. 1; ii. 7; 2 Tim. i. 1, 11; Titus i. 1.
[3] Eph. ii. 20.

ing passage already quoted¹ from the Book of Hebrews, which reads as follows: ⁽³⁾" How shall we escape, if we neglect so great salvation? which having at the first been spoken through the Lord, was confirmed unto us by them that heard; ⁽⁴⁾ God also bearing witness with them, both by signs and wonders, and by manifold powers, and by gifts of the Holy Ghost, according to his own will."² Another passage, comparing the words of the apostles to those of the prophets, is found in Second Peter: "That ye should remember the words which were spoken before by the holy prophets, and the commandment of the Lord and Saviour through your apostles."³

17. More specifically Paul calls upon the pretended prophets and spiritual teachers in Corinth to take knowledge of the things which he was writing unto them, that they are the commandment of the Lord.⁴ And in Galatians we find him emphatically saying: ⁽¹¹⁾ "For I make known to you, brethren, as touching the gospel which was preached by me, that it is not after man. ⁽¹²⁾ For neither did I receive it from man, nor was I taught it, but *it came to me* through revelation of Jesus Christ."⁵

18. In Second Peter there seems to be a dis-

---

¹ Paragraph 14.   ² Heb. ii. 3, 4.
³ 2 Peter iii. 2.   ⁴ 1 Cor. xiv. 37.
⁵ Gal. i. 11, 12.

tinct announcement of Paul's authority, in which the writer declares that in Paul's Epistles there "are some things hard to be understood, which the ignorant and unsteadfast wrest, as *they do* also the other Scriptures, unto their own destruction."[1] The noteworthy thing in this passage is that Paul's writings are compared with the *other Scriptures;* from which it follows that they had already attained the position of dignity and consideration accorded to the Old Testament.

19. At this point we are bound to notice a few exceptional passages, in which Paul seems to disclaim divine authority. In Rom. iii. 5 Paul says parenthetically, "I speak after the manner of men"; but this refers to the quotation from a supposed objector, whose sentiments he had introduced simply that he might refute them. In Rom. vi. 19 and Gal. iii. 15, the same phrase means that the apostle "uses language borrowed from common life, which may be easily understood."[2]

20. The seventh chapter of First Corinthians contains what seem at first to be more serious objections, but which wholly disappear upon close examination. Paul is here giving instructions concerning the behavior of married people upon points of conduct for which no absolute rule can be laid down. He therefore says in verse 6: "This I say by way of permission, not of com-

[1] 2 Peter iii. 15, 16.   [2] Stuart on Romans, p. 226.

mandment"; and in verse 12, having quoted from the words of Christ (whom he designates as the Lord), Paul adds: "But to the rest say I, not the Lord." In this, however, he does not disclaim apostolic authority, but simply indicates that his authority is in this case direct as touching a point of conduct concerning which Christ had not spoken. In verse 25, likewise, in giving commandment concerning virgins, he finds no special words of Christ which apply, and hence he gives his own judgment, "as one that hath obtained mercy of the Lord to be faithful." In the advice which follows, dissuading from marriage, it was not possible to lay down any unvarying rule; but no one would deny that, as a general thing, in such times of distress as the apostle's words indicate, contemplated marriage had better be deferred. Likewise, in the fortieth verse, the advice which the apostle gives to widows, respecting second marriage in the circumstances of the period, he says, "is after my judgment, and I think that I also have the Spirit of God." If Paul *thought* he had it, he doubtless did have it.

Passages in the eleventh and twelfth chapters of Second Corinthians are also thought by some to disclaim inspiration, — in some portions at least of the apostle's writings. Indeed, Rev. C. A. Row, a recent voluminous writer upon this subject, regards these chapters as by far the most important of all in proof of the alleged fact, that the apostle did not uniformly write "in virtue of the supernatural illumination which had been imparted to him"; but that he sometimes wrote "in his purely human character."[1] The passage which is conclusive to Dr. Row's mind is the following: "That which I speak, I speak not after the Lord, but as in foolishness, in this confidence of glorying."[2] Dr. Row is positive in his opinion that "to affirm that he [Paul] wrote passages of this kind at the dictation of the Divine Spirit, or as a record of his revelations, is to contradict his own express assertions." This positiveness, however, is entirely unwarranted, as a comprehensive examination of the context will clearly show. For in the eleventh and twelfth verses of the twelfth chapter the apostle specially emphasizes the authority with which he spoke, saying, that (11) "in nothing was I behind the very chiefest apostles, though I am nothing. (12) Truly the signs of an apostle were wrought among you in all patience, by signs and wonders and mighty works." This is preceded by the statement that the Corinthians had compelled him to become foolish, referring evidently to the foolishness spoken of in the preceding chapter. In view of this the literary character of the pas-

---

[1] See Revelation and Modern Theology Contrasted, pp. 113 ff.
[2] 2 Cor. xi. 17.

sages at once becomes evident. In general Paul condemns the practice of self-boasting, as not in accordance with the Lord's will. It is not a thing to be approved in itself; but circumstances compel him to make an exception to the rule, and seemingly to speak in a boastful spirit; and this he does; but it is their perverseness that compels him to this seeming folly. Thus a tone of mild irony is given to the passage; and no inference can be drawn from it adverse to the ordinary doctrine of inspiration. In this light the best interpreters have always regarded it.

21. Returning to the positive evidence, we note that in the Book of Revelation John declares that he was "in the Spirit on the Lord's day"[1] when he heard the great voice, and that he was told to write it "in a book, and send it to the seven churches"; and again, Revelation closes by pronouncing woes upon those who shall either add to or take from the words of the book of this prophecy.[2]

22. To comprehend the full meaning of the fact (referred to above)[3] that Peter speaks of Paul's writings as of equal authority with "other Scriptures," it is necessary at this point to consider the place which Old Testament Scriptures had in the esteem of the primitive believers. This will also aid us to understand both the scope of the promises of

---

[1] Rev. i. 10, 11. [2] Rev. xxii. 18, 19. [3] Paragraph 18.

inspiration given by Christ to his disciples, and the significance of the apostolic claims respecting the authority of their words.

The last four verses of the third chapter of Second Timothy furnish an appropriate introduction to a brief study of the question concerning the authority rightfully to be ascribed to the Old Testament: $^{(14)}$ "But abide thou in the things which thou hast learned and hast been assured of, knowing of whom thou hast learned them. $^{(15)}$ And that from a babe thou hast known the sacred writings [ἱερὰ γράμματα] which are able to make thee wise unto salvation through faith which is in Christ Jesus. $^{(16)}$ Every Scripture [πᾶσα γραφή] inspired of God [θεόπνευστος] is also profitable for teaching, for reproof, for correction, for instruction which is in righteousness: $^{(17)}$ that the man of God may be complete, furnished completely unto every good work."

Scholars are not agreed as to the translation of the sixteenth verse in this quotation. The more natural rendering would be, "All Scripture is inspired and profitable," making it a direct assertion of the inspiration of the Old Testament. But there is not so much depending upon this translation as is often supposed and represented. Taking it as it is in the Revised Version, we have the divine authority of the whole Old Testament both assumed and asserted in a most emphatic manner.

The inspiration of the Scripture referred to was not questioned either by Timothy or any other pious Jew. This we will presently show. It is a very important assertion, then, which is made when it is said that *every portion* of this Scripture is profitable.

Examining the passage in detail, we notice in verse 14 that Timothy is exhorted to abide in the things which he had learned and of which he had been assured, knowing of whom he had learned them. This is an assertion of Paul's own authority, for he was Timothy's instructor in Christianity. In verse 15 Paul asserts that the sacred writings (ἱερὰ γράμματα) in which Timothy had been instructed were able to make him "wise unto salvation, through faith which is in Christ Jesus." There can be no question that the "sacred writings" in verse 15 and "every Scripture" in verse 16 refer to the same thing.

What, now, is this to which they refer?

23. There are in the New Testament more than six hundred instances in which expressions have been incorporated into it from the Old Testament. But in the majority of cases these are simply appropriations of language, such as one writer might make from another, — indicating no more than great respect and familiarity. These are, however, important as showing the extent to which the thoughts in the New Testament are cast in the

forms of the Old. For example, the words of Mary, the mother of Jesus, in response to Elizabeth's salutation,[1] are largely made up of sentences from the Old Testament which would be applicable to the experience of any afflicted person to whom the Lord had shown great mercy.

24. There is, however, another class of quotations, which are introduced in such a manner that divine authority is ascribed specifically to the Old Testament, both in its parts and as a whole. The phrases in which this authority is ascribed are various, and illustrate all the more by their variety the pervasiveness of the sentiment which ascribed divine authority to the Old Testament. Sometimes the quotation is introduced by the phrase "It is written"; which does not mean merely that it was written somewhere, by somebody, but, as the context will show, it was authoritatively written; and the quotations introduced by this phrase are always from some book of the Old Testament as we now have it. Again, the quotations are frequently introduced by the phrases "It was written by the prophet," "It was spoken of the Lord by the prophet," "It was written by the prophet or prophets,"— sometimes mentioning them by name, and sometimes not. Again, when the commandments of the Old Testament are quoted, Christ, according to one evangelist,[2] introduces them as

[1] Luke i. 51–55.   [2] Matt. xv. 4.

what "*God* said"; according to another,[1] as what "*Moses* said." Again, a quotation is variously introduced as being the "prophecy of Isaiah,"[2] or as what "Isaiah said,"[3] or as what the "Holy Ghost spake by Isaiah the prophet."[4] For example, Ex. iii. 6 is referred to in Matt. xxii. 31 and Mark xii. 26 as what was "spoken by God"; in Luke xx. 37, as something which "Moses shewed." In the same manner Christ, according to Matthew[5] and Mark,[6] quotes the one hundred and tenth Psalm as what David said in the Spirit or by the Holy Ghost; while, according to Luke,[7] Christ refers to it as something David himself had said in the Book of Psalms; and in Heb. i. 13 God himself is said to have spoken the words. Ex. xxxiii. 19 is quoted by Paul[8] as what *God* said to Moses; while Ex. ix. 16, which contains God's direct address to Pharaoh, is introduced by Paul[9] as what the *Scripture* saith. Lev. xviii. 5 is a direct address of God to the people; Paul[10] introduces it, however, as something which Moses had said. Deut. xxxii. 21 is represented as what God said; Paul[11] introduces it as what Moses said. 1 Kings xix. 18 is endorsed by Paul[12] as what God said unto Elijah. Other places where New Testa-

---

[1] Mark vii. 10.   [2] Matt. xiii. 14.   [3] John xii. 39.
[4] Acts xxviii. 25.   [5] Matt. xxii. 43.   [6] Mark xii. 36.
[7] Luke xx. 42.   [8] Rom. ix. 15.   [9] Rom. ix. 17.
[10] Rom. x. 5.   [11] Rom. x. 19.   [12] Rom. xi. 4.

ment writers introduce Old Testament passages as words that were spoken by God, are Rom. xv. 10 and 2 Cor. vi. 16. Throughout the Book of Hebrews the numerous quotations from the Old Testament are, almost without exception, introduced as the direct words of God, with no allusion to the individual writers.[1]

25. In more than fifty places in the New Testament an appeal is made to "the Scripture" or "the Scriptures" in such a way as to show that those words were as definite in their meaning then as they are now among evangelical Protestants. Indeed, the words ἡ γραφή (*hee graphee*) and αἱ γραφαί (*hai graphai*) are used in the New Testament with all the varied shades of meaning in which we now employ the words "Scripture" and "Scriptures." The etymology of the word has ceased to define its meaning, and it signifies not any *writing* or *writings* in general, but a specific class of writings possessing divine authority. To them as such Christ and the apostles appeal with the utmost confidence as being within their sphere, when properly interpreted, final and infallible authority. This will appear from an inspection of the usage. In more than fifty places in the New Testament, as already remarked, an appeal is made to the *Scripture* or *Scriptures* as an authority which must

---

[1] See Heb. i. 6, 7, 8; ii. 12; iii. 7; iv. 3, 4; v. 6; x. 5, 15; xii. 26; xiii. 5.

be final. For example, in Mark xii. 10, 11 Jesus, in appropriating a portion of the one hundred and eighteenth Psalm, asks in an impassioned address: "Have ye not read even this Scripture: The stone which the builders rejected," etc? In the parallel passage in Matthew the plural is used, "Did ye never read in the Scriptures?"[1] while in Luke the quotation is introduced simply by the phrase, "What then is this that is written?"[2] In John vii. 40-43 the multitudes dispute concerning the authoritative claims put forth by Christ; and his opponents, supposing he came out of Galilee, appeal to "the Scripture" to prove that the Christ was to have been born in Bethlehem. Again, in John x. 35 Christ confutes his adversaries by quoting and interpreting a portion of the Old Testament, and enforces his argument by the assertion that "the Scripture cannot be broken." In John xix. 24, 28, 36, and 37 it is said that the parting of the Saviour's raiment among the soldiers, his cry for drink, the failure to break his bones, and the piercing of his side, each and all took place in order that the Scripture should be fulfilled. In John xx. 9 we read that the disciples did not yet know "the Scripture, that he must rise again from the dead." In Acts i. 16 Peter assures the other disciples that the death of Judas was a needful fulfilment of Scripture "which the Holy Ghost

---

[1] Matt. xxi. 42.   [2] Luke xx. 17.

spake before by the mouth of David." In Acts viii. 35 Philip begins "from this Scripture"[1] which the eunuch was reading, and preaches to him Jesus. In Rom. iv. 3; ix. 17; x. 11 the apostle appeals to what the Scripture saith, to convince his readers of the truth of the doctrines he is presenting. In Rom. xi. 2 a quotation from 1 Kings xix. 10, 14 is referred to as what the "Scripture saith of Elijah." Gal. iii. 8 speaks of the Scripture as preaching the gospel beforehand unto Abraham,[2] and verse 22 speaks of the Scripture as having shut up all under sin (that is, proved that all men are sinners, in need of God's grace). Another appeal to the Scripture, where the reference is to Genesis,[3] is found in Gal. iv. 30. In 1 Tim. v. 18 Paul points his argument by saying that "the Scripture saith, Thou shalt not muzzle the ox when he treadeth out the corn.[4] And, The laborer is worthy of his hire." This passage is thought by some to quote Luke as a part of Sacred Scripture; since the second clause of the quotation is not found in the Old Testament, but it occurs in Luke x. 7. In 2 Tim. iii. 16 we find the passage (already quoted)[5] to the understanding of which the present part of our discussion pertains. Following the Revised Version it reads: "Every Scripture inspired of God is also

[1] Isa. liii. 7.   [2] Gen. xii. 3.   [3] Gen. xxi. 10, 12.
[4] Deut. xxv. 4.   [5] Paragraph 22.

profitable for teaching, for reproof, for correction, for instruction which is in righteousness." Even with this rendering, it would be wholly unwarranted to infer that any portion of Scripture was regarded as uninspired. The object is to state the profitableness of such Scripture for teaching, etc., and that every part of it was profitable because inspired. In Jas. ii. 8, 23; iv. 5 quotations are introduced from Leviticus,[1] Genesis,[2] and Ecclesiastes,[3] with the assertions that these are "according to the Scripture," "fulfil the Scripture," or "what the Scripture saith." In 1 Peter ii. 6 quotations from Isaiah[4] and Psalms[5] are introduced as "contained in Scripture." In 2 Peter i. 20 we are told that "no prophecy of Scripture is of private interpretation," and that "no prophecy ever came by the will of man; but men spake from God, being moved by the Holy Ghost."

In all these instances the singular number is used, and in nearly every case the definite article is present, indicating that the writing referred to is to be distinguished from other writings. "The singular is employed merely in reference to the whole collection in its unity." The writings, though not bound together in one book in ancient times, were bound together in thought by the pervading element of divine

---

[1] Lev. xix. 18. [2] Gen. xv. 6. [3] Eccl. iv. 4.
[4] Isa. xxviii. 16. [5] Ps. cxviii. 22.

authority which pertained to them all; and this idea of divine authority separated them from all other writings.

26. In opposition to the views here presented, it is maintained by some,[1] that where the singular form of the word "Scripture" is used (as in the passages quoted), the reference is not to the Scripture as a whole, but to a particular part of the Scripture. Such persons would account for the uniform presence of the article by supposing that the writer meant in each case to limit his assertion to the particular passage quoted. This, however, is certainly an erroneous view, arising from an incomplete examination of the cases. It is true, as Lightfoot says, that we occasionally have the expressions "another Scripture,"[2] "this Scripture,"[3] "every Scripture";[4] but even these cases do not prove the point. The sacredness of a well-known and specific body of writings is implied and assumed, and the specific element of sacredness is still in the word. "Another Scripture" is equivalent to "another part of Scripture." In our language there is an analogous use in the word "hymn"; and we might write "as the hymn says"; in which case, unless we had mentioned some collection like the Vedic hymns, no one would understand us to refer to anything except to a well-

---

[1] Lightfoot on Gal. iii. 23.
[2] John xix. 37.
[3] Luke iv. 21.
[4] 2 Tim. iii. 16.

known body of hymns having some specific character which is assumed to be in the minds of those addressed. The specific sacred character of the writing referred to as ἡ γραφή (the Scripture) is unquestionable in the majority of cases, and those furnish the rule.[1] The exceptions noticed really prove the rule when properly considered. The use of the article to indicate that the specific characteristics of an individual are made prominent, is so familiar as not to demand extended illustration. When we say "the ox knoweth his owner,"[2] we do not necessarily mean any particular ox; but the use of the article throws into prominence the specific element giving character to all oxen. If we use the definite article to indicate some particular ox there must be something in the immediate connection to indicate the fact. The correctness of this view will be even more apparent when, a little later,[3] we shall consider the external evidence proving that the Jews in the time of Christ had as well-defined ideas of the character and limitations of the Old Testament as we have to-day.

27. The references of the New Testament to

---

[1] Let the reader examine the following references: John ii. 22; vii. 38, 42; x. 35; xix. 28; Acts viii. 32; Rom. iv. 3; ix. 17; x. 11; xi. 2; Gal. iii. 8, 22; iv. 30; 1 Tim. v. 18; 1 Peter ii. 6; 2 Peter i. 20.

[2] Isa. i. 3.

[3] See Chapter iv.

the Scriptures in the plural are also numerous, and are scarcely to be distinguished from those references which regard the whole collection in its unity. We read in Matthew: "Did ye never read in the Scriptures?"[1] "Ye do err, not knowing the Scriptures, nor the power of God";[2] "How, then, should the Scriptures be fulfilled, that thus it must be?"[3] "But all this is come to pass, that the Scriptures of the Prophets might be fulfilled";[4] where it is not the intention to intimate that some Scriptures were not of the Prophets, but rather that all the Scriptures were of prophetical origin. In Luke xxiv. 27 we are told that Christ, "beginning from Moses and from all the Prophets, interpreted to them in all the Scriptures the things concerning himself." In verses 44 and 45, in his parting words with his disciples, Christ reaffirms, that "all things must needs be fulfilled, which are written in the Law of Moses, and the Prophets, and the Psalms, concerning me," where the ordinary Jewish threefold division of the Old Testament Scriptures is indicated,— the Psalms being the first and most important part of the third division. In John v: 39 Jesus tells his hearers, that they search the Scriptures, because they think that in them they have eternal life; and adds, that "these are they which bear witness of me." In Acts xvii.

---

[1] Matt. xxi. 42.
[2] Matt. xxii. 29.
[3] Matt. xxvi. 54.
[4] Matt. xxvi. 56.

11 the Jews of Berea are said to be more noble than those of Thessalonica, because not only did they receive the word with all readiness of mind, but they examined the Scriptures daily, whether these things were so; and in xviii. 24, 28 we are told that Apollos was " mighty in the Scriptures," and that " he powerfully confuted the Jews [at Ephesus], *and that* publicly, shewing by the Scriptures that Jesus was the Christ." In Rom. i. 2 Paul refers to the gospel of God as something which God had "promised afore by his prophets in the Holy Scriptures." In Rom. xv. 4 we read : " For whatsoever things were written aforetime were written for our learning, that through patience and through comfort of the Scriptures we might have hope."

In Rom. xvi. 26 occurs again the phrase " Scriptures of the Prophets " already remarked upon in Matt. xxvi. 56. In 1 Cor. xv. 3, 4 Paul declares, (3) "I delivered unto you first of all that which also I received, how that Christ died for our sins according to the Scriptures; (4) and that he was buried; and that he hath been raised on the third day according to the Scriptures."

In 2 Peter iii. 16, as we have already remarked,[1] Peter sets Paul's writings over against *other* Scriptures, and so classes them together. As also in all his Epistles, speaking in them of these things,

[1] Paragraph 18.

wherein some are "hard to be understood, which the ignorant and unsteadfast wrest, as they do also the other Scriptures, unto their own destruction."

In glancing over this survey we perceive that by Christ and his apostles "everywhere and always the supreme authority of the sacred books is either directly asserted or conceded by implication. Scripture is the supreme arbiter, in all cases where a decision is required. The validity of the Redeemer's mission, and his claims, are tried by it; the doctrines which the apostles preached are tried by it; every virtue either of morality or piety is sanctioned by it."[1]

28. From a simple inspection of these New Testament references, the scholar would of necessity conclude that there was a well-known and definite collection of writings called "the Scripture" or "the Scriptures," written, indeed, by different persons, as Moses, David, Isaiah, Jeremiah, Hosea, Daniel; but that they all spoke with an authority higher than belonged to them in their personal relations. For example, in the parable of the rich man and Lazarus it is affirmed that if one will not hear Moses and the Prophets, neither will he be persuaded though one should rise from the dead.[2] He would infer, also, that these writings were divided

[1] Stuart on the Old Testament, p. 330.
[2] Luke xvi. 31.

into portions,[1] one of which was called the "Law," and another the "Prophets," and still another the "Psalms."[2] And on comparing these New Testament references with the literature extant in the time of Christ, he could, with only a small margin of error, determine, independently of external evidence, what writings were in the Saviour's time regarded as of a sacred character. It would appear that all but five or six of the books contained in our present Hebrew Bibles are quoted by the writers of the New Testament; and that no other writings are quoted in any such way as to imply their equal authority. "The New Testament writers could never have employed all these different appellations, and so often interchanged them without superadding any explanation, if the definite import of each and all had not been well understood by themselves and by those whom they addressed. The Old Testament must have been as definite then as it is now, and its limits as well known. Every Jew that could read must have known what books belonged to it, when copies of the Scriptures had become common."[3]

---

[1] Matt. xi. 13; xxii. 40; Luke xvi. 16; John i. 45; Acts xiii. 15; xxiv. 14; Rom. iii. 21. The same division is also indicated by the phrase "Moses and the Prophets" in Luke xvi. 29, 31; xxiv. 27; Acts xxviii. 23. "The Law, the Prophets, and the 'Psalms,'" Luke xxiv. 44.

[2] The ordinary name among the Jews for the third division of their Scriptures was *Hagiographa*, or Holy Writings, of which the Psalms were the first and principal division.

[3] Stuart on the Old Testament, pp. 255, 256.

29. The confinement of the quotations by Christ and the apostles to the books contained in the Old Testament, cannot have arisen from the lack of other writings from which to quote. Jewish literature extant in the time of Christ was abundant enough. There were the books still preserved in the Apocrypha (fourteen in number[1]); while in 2 Esdr. xiv. 46 no less than seventy apocryphal books are distinguished from the twenty-four canonical of the Hebrew Scriptures. There was also a large amount of what is called "apocalyptic" literature, prominent among which are the Book of Enoch, the Sibylline Oracles, the Apocalypse of Baruch, the Psalms of Solomon, the Assumption of Moses, the Ascension of Isaiah, the Book of Jubilees, all of which were probably in circulation in apostolic times. In addition to these there was an accumulating mass of rabbinical traditions, which soon after grew into the twelve massive volumes of the Talmud, consisting of minute and extended commentaries upon the various precepts of the Old Testament. So extensive is this literature that its neglect by Christ and the apostles cannot have been accidental. There is, indeed, a single reference in Jude (verse 14) to a passage in the Book of Enoch, as there are in Paul's writ-

[1] 1 and 2 Esdras, Tobit, Judith, Additions to Esther, Wisdom. Ecclesiasticus, Baruch with the Epistle of Jeremiah, the Song of the Three Children, the Story of Susanna, the Idol Bel and the Dragon, the Prayer of Manasses, and 1 and 2 Maccabees.

ings two or three allusions to the literature of Greece;[1] but these are scarcely more than illustrations.

30. Nor can the deference which Christ and the apostles paid to the Old Testament be accounted for on the so-called theory of accommodation, which implies that Christ humored the Jews of his time in their attachment to the Old Testament, for the sake of obtaining a favorable reception for the specific views which it was his main object to promulgate. This course of accommodation might be allowable in case the opinions encountered were comparatively unimportant, and sustained no vital relation to the main doctrines presented. For example, in ascribing the creation of the world to God, it might not be necessary to correct the prevalent ideas, erroneous though they were, concerning the motions by which astronomical phenomena are produced, or concerning the secondary processes through which the facts of geology have been brought about. The method of creation by divine power it may be impossible for finite beings ever to understand perfectly, and hence it will present for man a theme for endless study and a field for the perpetual enlargement of his knowledge. But the acknowledgment of God as Creator has a fundamental relation to all finite moral activity. Hence we need not expect to find in the

---

[1] Acts xvii. 28; Titus i. 12.

allusions of the inspired records to natural objects the discriminations appropriate to modern science; and, indeed, such discriminations are not to be found in the popular literature of our own day. With all the discoveries of modern science in our minds, we still use in our ordinary references to nature the language which describes it as it *appears* rather than such as expresses the obscure and hidden realities which modern science has proved to exist. We still speak of the "rising" and "setting" of the sun, the "waxing" and "waning" of the moon, as if ignorant of the facts of astronomy. But the references of Christ and the apostles to the Old Testament are of an entirely different character. The completion of the Old Testament in the New is a vital part of the New Testament itself. The types and prophecies of the Old Testament fulfilled in Christ are essential elements in defining to us Christ's nature and work. Furthermore, Christ in the most fearless manner set himself against various false views prevalent in his time concerning the Old Testament, and made a sharp distinction between the precepts of the law itself and the false interpretations which had become current in his time. The Sermon on the Mount is throughout a protest against current traditional misconceptions of the law, and Jesus did not hesitate on repeated occasions to enforce the spirituality of the law of the

Sabbath against the rabbinical interpretations of his day. Indeed, the whole New Testament, with its abundant and exclusive references to the Old Testament as of divine authority, is a protest against its acceptance in the narrow and literal sense in which the Jewish teachers of the time regarded it. We cannot therefore explain away, on the theory of accommodation, the apparent endorsement of the Old Testament by the writers of the New.

31. The repeated, emphatic, and exclusive appeal by the New Testament writers to the Old Testament Scriptures as when properly understood of divine authority, is the more impressive when we consider the manner in which the Old Testament writers both assume and assert their own divine commission. In numberless instances the writers of the Old Testament assume to speak in the name of the Lord. Moses expressly records that when he returned to be the leader of his people he did so by positive divine command, God saying to him, "Now therefore go, and I will be with thy mouth, and teach thee what thou shalt say."[1] Again, in Num. xvi. 28, Moses invokes a miracle, that the people might know that the Lord had sent him to do all these works, "for *I have* not *done them* of mine own mind." In Ex. xxxiv. 16 there is a command of God recorded forbidding in-

---

[1] Ex. iv. 12.

termarriage between the Israelites and the natives of Palestine. In Ezra ix. 1–4 there is record of a notorious breach of this command, and the author regards the transgression not merely as in defiance of the authority of Moses, but as in defiance of the "words of the God of Israel." Throughout the Pentateuch such phrases as "The Lord said unto Moses"; "These are the words which the Lord hath commanded"; "As the Lord commanded Moses"; "And the Lord called unto Moses, and spake unto him out of the tabernacle of the congregation, saying"; "This is it that the Lord spake, saying"; are too numerous to mention,— so numerous, indeed, that familiarity has caused them to lose much of their force. Nehemiah also speaks of "the book of the law of Moses, which the Lord had commanded to Israel."[1] The last words of David are introduced by the words, "The Spirit of the Lord spake by me, and his word was in my tongue."[2] In describing the vision which he saw concerning Judah and Jerusalem, the opening words of the prophet Isaiah are, "Hear, O heavens; and give ear, O earth; for the Lord hath spoken";[3] and Jeremiah introduces his prophecy with the phrase, "Then the word of the Lord came unto me, saying."[4] "Thus the commonly used language in reference to their own

[1] Neh. viii. 1.   [2] 2 Sam. xxiii. 2.
[3] Isa. i. 2.   [4] Jer. i. 4.

statements is: 'The mouth of the Lord hath spoken'; 'Thus saith the Lord'; 'Hear the word of the Lord.' And in numberless cases in the Old Testament prophets we find such expressions as these: 'The word that Isaiah the son of Amoz saw concerning Judah and Jerusalem'; 'The word that came to Jeremiah from the Lord, saying'; 'The word of the Lord came expressly to Ezekiel'; 'The beginning of the word of the Lord by Hosea'; 'Now the word of the Lord came unto Jonah the son of Amittai, saying'; 'The word of the Lord that came unto Micah'; 'The book of the vision of Nahum'; 'The burden which Habakkuk the prophet did see'; 'The word of the Lord which came unto Zephaniah'; 'In the first day of the month came the word of the Lord by Haggai the prophet'; 'In the eighth month came the word of the Lord unto Zechariah'; 'The burden of the word of the Lord to Israel by Malachi.'"[1]

The present state of our inquiry is this: We have seen, first, that the supernatural is so prominent in the main facts of Christianity that it ought to occasion no surprise to find it extending so as to guarantee the record of these facts;[2] secondly, that the promises of Christ that supernatural aid would be granted to the apostles to insure accuracy of memory and correctness in

---

[1] Bannerman on Inspiration, p. 310.   [2] See Chapter i.

foretelling future events, are explicit, and are confirmed by miraculous gifts;[1] and thirdly, that the apostles claimed to speak by the authority of the Holy Spirit, and that both they and the Saviour himself attest in superabundant measure the divine authority of the Old Testament. This they do (a) by directly adopting the views current at the time as to the sacredness of the Old Testament Scripture; (b) by repeatedly making various portions of it their final appeal in argument; (c) by direct assertions that portions, at least, of the Scripture were the direct word of God, or were spoken by the Holy Spirit; (d) by refraining from attempts to correct or criticise any portion of the Scripture then held sacred, though freely criticising the traditional views of their times. This establishes the divine authority of the Old Testament. To establish the authority of the books of the New Testament we have to prove that they were either written or endorsed by apostles, or, at any rate, that they correctly represent apostolic teachings and originated in apostolic times. They then become invested with the authority of the apostolic commission. A sufficient proof of such investiture of authority is that they were so received by the primitive church, who knew both the apostles and their doctrines, and who with the standard of Old Testament authority before them exalted the New

[1] See Chap. ii.

Testament to a co-ordinate place with the Old. But we are anticipating the results of a succeeding chapter.

It will now be in place to consider the important and somewhat difficult question, What books constitute the inspired record? a department of inquiry comprehended in the technical name of *Canonics.*

IV.

THE CANON OF THE OLD TESTAMENT.

32. THE technical words *canon* and *canonical* are so convenient that we cannot well avoid their use. The word *canon*, originally *a carpenter's rule*, is used in an active and a passive sense, Actively considered it is a rule according to which something is regulated; passively, it is that which is determined by the application of a rule. When applied to the Bible the noun is used in a passive sense, and indicates those books which have stood the tests applied by the early church to determine their authenticity and inspiration. When so received, the book becomes a part of the rule of faith in the active sense, that is, it becomes a positive and authoritative element in determining our standards of doctrine. Hence it is a matter of no small importance to determine the exact limits of the sacred canon. Nor is the task wholly free from difficulty.

33. There are a few books of the Old Testament to which no distinct reference is made by the writers of the New, among which are Esther, Ezra, Nehemiah, Ecclesiastes, and the Song of Solomon.

These however, we accept, as a part of the Old Testament, because of the evidence we have that at the beginning of our era they formed an integral portion of the Sacred Scriptures, and so received the endorsement of the general references of Christ and his apostles to the Old Testament as a whole. That the Sacred Scriptures to which Christ and his apostles refer, included the books just mentioned, and did not include the Apocrypha, is evident from a variety of considerations.

In Luke xxiv. 44 Christ refers to the Scriptures under the apparently well-known threefold division of the Law, the Prophets, and the Psalms. "In the twenty-seventh verse of the same chapter it is said of Jesus, that ' beginning from Moses and from the Prophets, he explained to them [his disciples] in all the Scriptures the things which concerned himself.' This passage is virtually the same with that above. Two divisions of Scripture are here alluded to by name, and the third is separated from them by a phraseology which necessarily imports that there were other portions of Scripture besides the two named, which Jesus interpreted for the disciples, as he first had done in respect to the Law and the Prophets. . . . That the Scriptures in a specific form are here meant, there can be no doubt; for after speaking of the things written in the Law, the Prophets, and the Psalms, concerning Christ, it is said of Jesus, that 'he opened the

THE CANON OF THE OLD TESTAMENT. 57

mind [of the disciples] to understand τὰς γραφάς, *the Scriptures'*; viz. those Scriptures which he had quoted and explained."[1] The arrangement of the books in the Hebrew Bible is as follows:[2]

I. THE LAW
- Genesis.
- Exodus.
- Leviticus.
- Numbers.
- Deuteronomy.

II. THE PROPHETS,
- Former
  - Joshua.
  - Judges.
  - 1 and 2 Samuel.
  - 1 and 2 Kings.
- Latter
  - Major
    - Isaiah.
    - Jeremiah.
    - Ezekiel.
  - Minor
    - The twelve minor Prophets.

III. THE WRITINGS,
- *a.*
  - Psalms.
  - Proverbs.
  - Job.
- *b.*
  - The Song of Songs.
  - Ruth.
  - Lamentations.
  - Ecclesiastes.
  - Esther.
- *c.*
  - Daniel.
  - Ezra.
  - Nehemiah.
  - 1 and 2 Chronicles.

In Matt. xxiii. 35 Christ refers to "the righteous blood shed on the earth, from the blood of Abel the righteous unto the blood of Zachariah, son of

---

[1] Stuart on the Old Testament, pp. 249, 250.
[2] See article Bible in Smith's Bible Dictionary.

Barachiah, whom ye slew between the sanctuary and the altar"; which are the first and last martyrs in that section of history of which we have an account in the Hebrew Scriptures; the last book in the Hebrew Scriptures being Second Chronicles, and the murder of Zachariah being recounted near the close of that book. The significance of this reference appears at a glance upon the preceding table.

34. The threefold division mentioned in paragraph 33, and appearing in the above table, is first referred to about the middle of the second century B. C., when the translator of the apocryphal BOOK OF ECCLESIASTICUS, otherwise called the WISDOM OF SIRACH, introduces his work by speaking of the devotion of his grandfather (the author of the book) to the reading of "the Law, and the Prophets, and *the other books* of our fathers"; and twice more in a short space this same author mentions the threefold division: once, as "the Law, and the Prophets, and *the other* [books] which follow after them"; and again, as "the Law, the Prophecies, and *the rest of the books*," where it is very evident, from the use of the article, that "*the* books," like our phrase "*the* Scriptures," does not mean books in general, but a specific and well-understood class of books of the same character with the Law and the Prophets. There is no sufficient ground for Dr. Ladd's asser-

tion that these titles of the third division given in the preface to Ecclesiasticus are less respectful than the other two; nor for the assertion that this apocryphal book "itself makes pretensions to prophetic and canonical significance."[1] Ecclesiasticus xxiv. 33 does indeed read, "I will yet pour out teaching as prophecy, and leave it to everlasting generations"; but, as the connection shows, the writer does not represent himself, but rather Wisdom (who is personified through the whole chapter), as the one who is to do this.

35. The testimony of various other books of the Apocrypha to the superior value of the writings included in our present Old Testament is likewise important. The books of the Apocrypha (which we have already enumerated)[2] were written subsequent to the time of Malachi (not far from 430 B. C.), and obtained currency in connection with the circulation of the Greek translation of the Old Testament called the "Septuagint." These apocryphal books number, as already said, fourteen. They make no distinct claims to divine authority. There is no certain evidence that any of them were quoted by Christ and his apostles. Neither of these facts, however, is absolutely decisive against their canonical authority, since the same is true of

---

[1] See Doctrine of Sacred Scripture, by George T. Ladd, D.D., Vol. I. p. 651.

[2] See paragraph 31, p. 50.

some of the books of the Old Testament, just mentioned; still, this absence of both the claim and recognition of divine authority is an important consideration when combined with certain other facts now to be mentioned.

The distinct testimony of the Apocrypha to the specially sacred character of the Old Testament is thus summarized by a most competent scholar:[1] "A peculiar authority is imputed in the Apocrypha to the canonical writings. They are held to be distinct from all other books, and given of God for human guidance, through prophets inspired for the purpose. They are called 'holy books,'[2] and their writers are represented to have been under the influence of the Holy Spirit.[3] It is distinctly said of Jeremiah in one place, that he was a prophet 'sanctified from the mother's womb.'[4] So in Baruch a passage is cited from this prophet with this formula, 'Thus saith the Lord.'[5] The common division of the Scriptures into Law and Prophets, too, shows that the authors of the several canonical books were looked upon as prophets, that is, as inspired men.[6] And what was true of the canonical books, in general, had special force as

---

[1] Prof. E. C. Bissell, Commentary on the Apocrypha, p. 44.
[2] 1 Macc. xii. 9.
[3] 1 Esd. i. 28; vi. 1; Ecclus. xlviii. 24.
[4] Ecclus. xlix. 7.
[5] Bar. ii. 21.
[6] Cf. Jos., *Contra Ap.*, i. 7.

THE CANON OF THE OLD TESTAMENT. 61

applied to the five books of Moses. No epithets were thought extravagant, no praise too high to be bestowed on him, the greatest of the prophets, and his divinely prompted, divinely acknowledged work. He was like the glorious angels and beloved of God and men.[1] The Mosaic code was the law of the Highest,[2] holy and God-given.[3] It was the sum total of all wisdom. 'All these things,' said the son of Sirach, 'are [true of] the Book of the Covenant of the most high God, the law which Moses commanded for an heritage to the congregations of Jacob. It gives fulness of wisdom as Pison, and as Tigris in the time of the new fruits. It maketh the understanding to abound like Euphrates, and as Jordan in the time of harvest. It maketh the doctrine of knowledge appear as the light and as Gihon [i.e. the Nile] in the time of vintage.'"[4]

36. The testimony of JOSEPHUS is even more explicit than that of the Apocrypha. And after making all the abatement possible, Josephus remains, when speaking of the customs and beliefs of the Jews of his time, a witness of the very highest authority. His father was a distinguished priest, and he himself received the best education of his people and time. At the age of nineteen he joined the sect of the Pharisees. His treatise

---

[1] Ecclus. xlix. 2.   [2] Ecclus. xlix. 4.
[3] 2 Macc. vi. 23.   [4] Ecclus. xxiv. 23-27.

against Apion was written in defence of his own religion against a violent attack made upon it by that celebrated grammarian of Alexandria. In this work Josephus says:

"For we [the Jews] have not an innumerable multitude of books among us, disagreeing from and contradicting one another [as the Greeks have], but only twenty-two books, which contain the records of all the past times; which are justly believed to be divine; and of them five belong to Moses, which contain his laws and the traditions of the origin of mankind till his death. This interval of time was little short of three thousand years; but as to the time from the death of Moses till the reign of Artaxerxes [the time of Nehemiah and Malachi], king of Persia, who reigned after Xerxes, the prophets, who were after Moses, wrote down what was done in their times in thirteen books. The remaining four books contain hymns to God and precepts for the conduct of human life. It is true, our history hath been written since Artaxerxes very particularly [referring to the Apocrypha], but hath not been esteemed of the like authority with the former by our forefathers, because there hath not been an exact succession of prophets since that time; and how firmly we have given credit to those books of our own nation, is evident by what we do; for during so many ages as have already passed, no one has been so bold as

THE CANON OF THE OLD TESTAMENT. 63

either to add anything to them, to take anything from them, or to make any change in them."[1]

To this testimony of Josephus, as already intimated, it may be objected, that he is not altogether a veracious writer, and that in preparing his own histories he himself used undue freedom with the same collections of writings which in this quotation he so highly extols. This inconsistency, however, can easily be accounted for, from the character and situation of the man, without throwing any discredit upon the present testimony to the esteem in which the Old Testament was held by the Jews of his time. The motives which led him in his historical works to jumble fact and fancy together, were not present in introducing such a reference to the belief of his fellow-countrymen concerning the Scripture as is here offered in evidence against Apion.

The reader might at first stumble over the fact that Josephus reckons the sacred books of the Jews as only twenty-two in number. This, however, conforms to the enumeration applied to the Jewish sacred books at the time, making the number agree with that of the letters in the Hebrew alphabet.[2] To bring about this conformity, First and Second Samuel, First and Second Kings, First and Second Chronicles are each reckoned as one

[1] Contra Apionem, i. 8.
[2] Cf. the subdivisions of Ps. cxix.

book; as also are Judges and Ruth, Ezra and Nehemiah, Jeremiah and his Lamentations, and the twelve minor Prophets. Josephus's testimony to the number of books regarded by the Jews as sacred is all the more weighty because in his histories he freely uses other literature, especially the apocryphal books, which in his treatise Against Apion he expressly excludes from the list of inspired writings.

37. The testimony of PHILO JUDÆUS, a learned Jew of Alexandria who wrote extensively about the beginning of the Christian era, confirms that of Josephus. While Philo does not give a catalogue of the books regarded as sacred by his contemporaries, he quotes, as books of divine origin, the Pentateuch, Joshua, First Samuel, Ezra, Isaiah, Jeremiah, Hosea, Zechariah, the Psalms, and the Proverbs, and makes a casual reference to Judges, Job, and First Kings,[1] but "from the Apocrypha he makes no excerpts or citation, not giving it the honor he accords to Plato, Hippocrates, and several other Greek writers."[2]

38. In the year 179 A. D., MELITO, bishop of Sardis, travelled extensively throughout the East, and procured for a friend "an exact statement of the Old Testament, how many in number, and in what

---

[1] Horne's Introduction, Vol. I. p. 42.
[2] Schaff-Herzog Encyclopædia of Religious Knowledge, article Canon, Vol. I. p. 386.

order the books were written."[1] His list agrees exactly with our present Old Testament, except that Nehemiah and Esther are wanting. Westcott, however, thinks they were probably included in the general title, "Esdras." A little later the learned ORIGEN prepared a similar list, enumerating the twenty-two books which the Hebrews hand down as included in the Old Testament. The fragment of Origen in which this is preserved, is doubtless somewhat imperfect, which may account for his omission of the twelve minor Prophets and his addition of the Epistle of Jeremiah. Origen expressly excludes the Maccabees from the canon.[2]

39. A little later still, JEROME, the greatest scholar of his age, and the reviser of the Latin translation of the Bible, gives a list of the canonical books of the Old Testament, agreeing exactly with that now received by Protestants, "adding that whatever is out of the number of these must be placed in the Apocrypha."[3] The TALMUD, which represents the continuous Jewish tradition, gives the same list.

40. That there should be an occasional quotation from the Apocrypha by the early church fathers is not surprising when we remember that in the Septuagint (the Greek translation so ex-

---

[1] Eusebius, Church History, iv. 26.
[2] Ibid., vi. 25.
[3] Prologue to Galatians.

tensively used about the beginning of our era), the canonical and the uncanonical books were published together in the same volume; as they are in many Bibles of the present, even when the difference between them is distinctly recognized. But even so, it was not till the close of the second century that any citations were made by the church fathers from the Apocrypha which would seem to imply its canonical character; and even then it would appear that they acknowledged it inadvertently, "with no intention of giving them [the apocryphal books] a theological significance and endorsement which should be valid for subsequent times."[1] In proportion to its size the Apocrypha was quoted far less frequently than the canonical Scriptures. The supposed citations from the Apocrypha in the recently discovered Teaching of the Apostles (Διδαχή τῶν Ἀποστόλων) are no exception, even though its date be assigned to the early part of the second century. With one exception the correspondences are of the vaguest kind, and do not compare at all with the distinct and numerous references of the New Testament to the Old.

41. The judgment of sound scholarship upon this subject is well expressed by the eminent student of the Apocrypha from whom we have just quoted. After remarking that until the Council of Trent not even the Roman Catholic church had

[1] Bissell on the Apocrypha, p. 51.

given the Apocrypha authoritative recognition, and that it "was the criticisms of Protestants, particularly of Erasmus and Luther, on the loose practice of Romanists respecting the Bible, that led to a consideration of the subject at this time,"[1] he adds: "It is obvious that this important step was taken by the Council of Trent for other than simple historical reasons. Without doubt one of these was to emphasize, as much as possible, the differences existing between themselves and the Protestants as represented by their two great leaders, Erasmus and Luther. In fact, this purpose was openly announced by Cardinal Polus. Another reason is to be found in the weighty circumstance that the apocryphal books might be found very useful, if not, indeed, absolutely essential, in defending certain peculiar dogmas of the Romish church, as, for instance, that of the intercession of angels,[2] and of departed saints,[3] of the merit of good works,[4] its teaching concerning purgatory, and the desirability that the living pray for the dead.[5] Tanner candidly acknowledges, indeed, that the Apocrypha were pronounced canonical because the 'church found its own spirit in these books.' Still further, it was a matter of no little interest to maintain at all hazards the

---

[1] Apocrypha, pp. 52, 53.
[2] Tob. xii. 12.
[3] 2 Macc. xv. 14; cf. Bar. iii. 4.
[4] Tob. iv. 7; Ecclus. iii. 30.
[5] 2 Macc. xii. 42 ff.

dignity of the Vulgate, and this would have been greatly imperilled if, on the authority of a general council, so large a part of it as was contained in the Old Testament Apocrypha was declared to be of inferior value. But if none of these reasons considered separately, or when taken together, could be regarded as sufficient to determine the action of the council with reference to the Scriptures, there is another whose weight cannot be disputed. It is the principle that then dominated, and must ever dominate in such a system as the Romish church represents, namely, that there are no distinct periods of divine revelation, but that it is an uninterrupted process going forward in and through the church. 'When, therefore, the Catholic church insists with special emphasis on the full and equal canonicity of the Apocrypha, its interest in them, before all, declares itself for the reason that by their means the gaps in the inspired literature are filled up and that continuity [*Solidarität*] of canonical development restored, which, in turn, forms the innermost idea of the dogma of tradition.'"[1]

[1] Bissell on the Apocrypha, p. 54.

V.

THE CANON OF THE NEW TESTAMENT.

42. At first thought it is a puzzling fact that the canon of Sacred Scripture was not determined for the church, once for all, by the formal act of any authoritative ecclesiastical body. The Bible was of gradual growth. The supernatural history of Israel, of which the Old Testament is a product, closed four centuries before the Christian era; and it is acknowledged on all hands that from that time to the birth of Christ there were no prophets in Israel. And more and more the people were learning to prize their sacred history, when about two hundred years before the beginning of our era the fearful persecutions of Antiochus Epiphanes brought out this latent judgment of the church into those definite forms of testimony which we have been considering. A similar persecution of the Christian church under Diocletian (beginning about A. D. 304) brought out into definite and convincing shape the evidence respecting the New Testament canon. Under this emperor it was enacted (A. D. 303), among other things, that

"the bishops and presbyters should deliver all their sacred books into the hands of the magistrates; who were commanded, under the severest penalties, to burn them in a public and solemn manner."[1] A long-continued and ferocious period of persecution followed.[2] All who delivered up their copies of Scripture to destruction were excommunicated from the church.[3] At a later time "the question of the readmission of these traitors *(traditores)*, as they were emphatically called, created a schism in the church."[4] Many, however, deceived the government by palming off the writings of heretics upon the officers. Such were afterwards terribly maltreated by the pagans.

The catalogue of the New Testament prepared soon after this by Eusebius,[5] reckons as canonical beyond dispute the four Gospels, the Acts, fourteen Epistles of Paul (which would include Hebrews), First Epistle of John, the First of Peter, and "if proper" the Revelation of John. Among disputed books at that time Eusebius reckons James, Jude, Second Epistle of Peter, the Second and Third of John, and distinctly pronounces all others spurious. Other private cata-

---

[1] Gibbon's Decline and Fall of the Roman Empire, Chap. xvi.
[2] For particulars, see Eusebius's Church History, Book viii.
[3] Eusebius' Church History and Lactantius' Institutes.
[4] Westcott in Smith's Bible Dictionary, article Canon.
[5] Church History, iii. 25.

logues were prepared during this century by Athanasius, Jerome, and Augustine, each of whom reckons all the books of the New Testament as canonical; and after the close of the fourth century there is practical unanimity upon the subject.

43. Interest, however, concentrates upon the evidence borne concerning the canonical authority of the books of the New Testament during the second and third centuries, — a period in such close proximity to the apostolic age that its history is of pre-eminent value in every department of Christian evidences.[1] The apostle John was alive near the close of the first century. The contemporaries of John, some of whom received personal instruction from " the beloved disciple," were the teachers of the great defenders of the Christian faith whose names are prominent about the close of the second century. The various testimonies adduced from this period concerning the canonical authority of the individual books of the New Testament, receive weight from several considerations: *a*. It is the testimony not of individuals, but of the common consent of great numbers of Christian believers. The writers speak for their class. *b*. Much of the evidence is incidental, so as to exclude the theory of its being manufactured. It is the appeal of writers, both for and against Christianity, to authorities which no one thought of disputing.

[1] See the author's Logic of Christian Evidences, p. 229 sq.

c. The testimony is widely distributed, and is that of Christian communities in France, in Italy, in Northern Africa, in Egypt, in Asia Minor, and Mesopotamia, — a testimony as widespread as the Roman empire. From Lyons in France to Edessa in Mesopotamia, the distance in a straight line is twenty-five hundred miles; and Alexandria is fourteen hundred miles from Carthage, and a thousand miles from Edessa. Communication was then extremely slow and difficult. The Christian communities spoke different languages, and their outward circumstances were as diverse as can well be imagined. These facts combined give irresistible force to the testimony of the period under consideration concerning the early records of Christianity. It is evident at a glance that the testimonies of the different bodies of Christians scattered over this wide area, would not each be equally clear concerning every portion of Sacred Scripture.

44. The proper witnesses to the canonical authority of the books of the New Testament, are the Christian communities to whom they were first addressed, and among whom they were first circulated. The whole condition and experience of these early communities fitted them to pass judgment upon the internal marks of apostolic authorship. These communities were under the pressure of every conceivable motive to be on their guard

against imposition. They knew the signature and style of the apostles and their companions, and were familiar at first hand with the whole circle of apostolic doctrines. Furthermore, if we believe in a Providence at all, it would seem clear that God, who cares for the sparrow's fall and numbers the hairs of our head, would not leave without adequate record and witness the expensive revelation made through the incarnation and death of his Son.

45. What now are the facts concerning the books of the New Testament as they emerge to historical recognition about the close of the second and the beginning of the third century? *a.* A translation of the writings upon which the faith of the church was founded, was made into the SYRIAC language some time during the second century, and was in authoritative circulation in the valley of the Euphrates. This translation contains all of our present New Testament except Jude, Second Peter, Second and Third John, and the Revelation, and no other books.

b. About the same time translations appear in the LATIN, and are in circulation in Northern Africa and Italy. A catalogue of New Testament books known as the MURATORIAN CANON, prepared about the year 170, has been preserved, and well represents the limits assigned to the sacred writings by the churches in Northern Africa and Italy. This catalogue includes the four Gospels, Acts, the thirteen Epistles of Paul, First and Second John, Jude, and Revelation. Combining these two catalogues, we have distinct documentary evidence of the canonical recognition by the churches of the second century of every book of the New Testament except Second Peter.

c. The great commentators and writers whose labors begin at this period, make constant appeals to the sacred writings which embody the facts and doctrines of Christianity. The quotations of these great apologists and commentators from individual books incidentally show that they received as canonical, and as of equal value with the Old Testament, nearly every book now included in the New Testament; but as to a few books the manner of quotation is indecisive. The quotations from the books enumerated in the catalogues just presented[1] (and in which they agree) are so numerous, and the references to them on all hands are so explicit and definite, that we need not accumulate the testimony. There is no reasonable question touching the canonicity of the four Gospels, Acts, Paul's Epistles, First Peter, and First John.

d. There are, however, seven books of the present canon to which the universal consent of Christian believers had not been explicitly obtained at the close of the second century. These books

---

[1] Paragraphs 43 and 45 *b.*

are Hebrews, Jude, James, Second and Third John, Second Peter, and the Revelation. Besides these, there are four works of early writers which were treated with a good deal of consideration during the second and third centuries, but which were never received as canonical. These are the Epistle of Barnabas, the Shepherd of Hermas, the Epistle of Clement, and the Apocalypse of Peter. We will give the testimony concerning these in detail.

46. The evidence in favor of the EPISTLE TO THE HEBREWS is as follows: *a.* It was included in the Syriac Version, referred to in paragraph 45. This version contained no other disputed book.

b. The teachers in the catechetical school of Alexandria without exception received it as canonical, though expressing doubts as to its authorship. The weight of this testimony will appear upon noticing that at that period Alexandria was the centre of the Greek-speaking Jews, and that PANTÆNUS, who ascribed the Epistle to Paul, was at the head of the catechetical school of Alexandria about the year 150, and *c.* that his pupil CLEMENT OF ALEXANDRIA (about 200), who succeeded Pantænus in the school, unhesitatingly acknowledges the canonical authority of the book and its relations to Paul as author; accounting for its peculiarities of style on the theory that Luke had translated it from Hebrew.[1] *d.* A little later ORIGEN, who had been a pupil of both Pantænus and Clement, became an instructor in this catechetical school of Alexandria. He frequently quotes the Book of Hebrews,[2] as a genuine Epistle of Paul; and though at times he expresses doubt as to its authorship, he never questions its canonical authority. It should be observed that the recognition of Hebrews here adduced, is from that portion of the church best competent to decide upon its authenticity. On the other hand, in the Western churches there is a lack of evidence supporting the claims of Hebrews to canonical authority. The Muratorian Canon[3] (A.D. 170) did not originally contain it. TERTULLIAN (A.D. 220) acknowledges the Epistle as of great authority, and ascribes it to Barnabas. IRENÆUS, bishop of Lyons, France (about A.D. 175), rarely, if ever, refers to the Epistle. All this, however, is negative evidence, and can be accounted for by the distance separating the churches where these writers lived from the region where the Epistle was first circulated, or from the difficulty which Latin Christians would have in appreciating thoughts clothed in such exclusive Jewish dress as we find in the Book of Hebrews. The hesitation of the Western churches respecting the Book of Hebrews reveals,

---

[1] Eusebius, Church History, vi. 14.
[2] Ibid., vi. 25.   [3] Paragraph 45 *b.*

however, the ordinary caution upon which the early believers acted.

47. The EPISTLE OF JUDE is included in the Muratorian Canon (170), though doubts are expressed as to whether Jude were the author. Clement of Alexandria, Origen, and Tertullian recognized it as canonical, though in one place Origen alludes to a doubt. On the other hand, it is absent in the Syriac Version, and there is no trace of it in the " Asiatic churches up to the commencement of the fourth century."

48. The EPISTLE OF JAMES is found in the Syriac Version, and, according to Eusebius, was publicly read in most of the churches as genuine at the beginning of the fourth century;[1] and is quoted as canonical " by almost all the fathers of the fourth century." On the other hand, it is absent from the Muratorian Canon, and is but indistinctly referred to by Irenæus.

Jude describes himself as the brother of James. It is doubtful whether they were apostles, or the brothers of Christ mentioned in Matt. xiii. 55, who were of course companions of the apostles, and one of whom was pastor of the church at Jerusalem.[2]

49. The SECOND and THIRD EPISTLES OF JOHN are so short that it is not surprising to find less evidence respecting them than respecting the longer and more characteristic portions. But, according

[1] Church Hist., ii. 23.   [2] Acts xv. 13.

to Westcott, "they were included in the Old Latin Version [in existence during the second century]. Clement of Alexandria wrote short notes upon them. Irenæus quotes the Second Epistle as St. John's."[1] These Epistles also closely resemble the First Epistle in their language.

50. The SECOND EPISTLE OF PETER. The amount of direct evidence to substantiate the canonical authority of this Epistle is less than that of any other portion of Scripture. There is no distinct evidence of its having " been referred to by any author earlier than Origen" (about 220); though Clement of Alexandria is reported by the church historians Eusebius and Photius to have written a "commentary upon all the disputed Epistles, in which this was certainly included." In the fourth century Didymus, a celebrated writer of Alexandria, refers frequently to the Epistle. We may safely adopt the words of Canon Cook concerning it: "The historical evidence is certainly inconclusive, but not such as to require or to warrant the rejection of the Epistle. The silence of the fathers is accounted for more easily than its admission into the canon after the question as to its genuineness had been raised. It is not conceivable that it should have been received without positive attestation from the churches to which it was first addressed. We know that the autographs of

---

[1] Epistles of St. John, Introduction, p. liv.

apostolic writings were preserved with care. It must also be observed that all motive for forgery is absent. This Epistle does not support any hierarchical pretensions, nor does it bear upon any controversies of a later age."[1] If Second Peter is not genuine it is a bare forgery; for it professes to come from Peter, " an apostle of Jesus Christ,"[2] and to be a " second Epistle."[3]

51. The REVELATION OF JOHN claims to have been written by the apostle of that name;[4] for, though there may have been many bearing the name of John, there could have been but one who could describes himself as the " servant John, who bare witness of the word of God, and of the testimony of Jesus Christ, even of all things that he saw,"[5] and who could at that time, in Asia, where the apostle was so well known, assume the authoritative tone pervading the book. It could not have been an easy matter for such a book as Revelation to have been so generally received, as it was early in the second century, as a product of the apostle John unless it claimed to be genuine, and unless that claim could be well supported. Yet we find that JUSTIN MARTYR, who was born about the time of the death of John, and suffered martyrdom about 165, distinctly ascribes the book to the apos-

---

[1] Smith's Bible Dict., article Peter.
[2] i. 1.   [3] iii. 1.   [4] Chap. i. 1–9; xxii. 8, 9.
[5] Cf. John i. 14; xix. 35; 1 John i. 2.

tle John, as does the Muratorian Canon; while Irenæus (about 175) often quotes the book as the work of John, as does Clement of Alexandria (200); and Origen (220) expressly says the apostle John wrote the Revelation. The arguments against its apostolic origin are chiefly drawn: *a.* from the doubts expressed upon the point by Dionysius,[1] a bishop of Alexandria (about 240); *b.* from its not being found in the Syriac Version, and *c.* from the character and literary style of its contents. Indeed, it was this last consideration which seemed to have induced the doubts expressed by Dionysius. "Jerome states that the Greek churches felt with respect to the Revelation a similar doubt to that of the Latins respecting the Epistle to the Hebrews."[2] The positive testimony for its canonical authority, however, is so overwhelming that negative testimony and the expression of doubts, which can be readily accounted for by the difficulties which the book raises in the minds of interpreters, should have little weight in discrediting the book, and, as in the case of Hebrews, the doubts entertained for a time by a portion of the churches increase the confidence with which we accept their final decision.

52. The judgment of the early churches regarding the canonical character of the books of the

---

[1] Eusebius, Church Hist., vii. 25.
[2] Smith's Bible Dict., article Revelation.

New Testament as now received, is confirmed by the general character of the New Testament apocryphal literature. There were about fifty apocryphal Gospels, all of which may, as far as we know them, be pronounced absolutely worthless. There were several imitations of the Book of Acts, as also of various Epistles and the Revelation, none of which succeeded in deceiving the churches. The EPISTLE OF BARNABAS, however, was received by the old Greek church as genuine, but not canonical, and was quoted seven times by Clement of Alexandria and three times by Origen. This was also found complete at the end of the celebrated CODEX SINAITICUS.[1] But it never received canonical recognition, or much attention, and is now generally supposed to have been written during the second century.

53. The SHEPHERD OF HERMAS, called by Dean Stanley "the Pilgrim's Progress of the church of the second century," was certainly held in very high esteem at that time. It is quoted by Irenæus, Clement of Alexandria, and Origen, and is found in connection with the Epistle of Barnabas at the end of the Codex Sinaiticus, just referred to. The Muratorian Canon also speaks of it, but says it was for private reading only. And there is nowhere any distinct acknowledgment of it as canonical; while both Tertullian and Eusebius

[1] See below, paragraph 57.

clearly reject it. Its being bound with some of the earliest copies of the New Testament has probably no greater significance than a similar treatment bestowed upon the Apocrypha of the Old Testament in a large portion of the Protestant churches at the present time.

54. The fact can scarcely have escaped the attention of the reader, that the books of the New Testament received by the early Christians as canonical are all attributed either directly or indirectly to the apostles. The books which do not bear the name of an apostle are still connected with the apostles by the close relation to the apostles of the writers to whom they are attributed.

MARK is with one consent represented by the earliest Christian writers as the interpreter of Peter. LUKE, the author of the third Gospel and of Acts, is with equal unanimity supposed to represent the views of Paul. The EPISTLE TO THE HEBREWS, if not attributed to Paul, is supposed to have been written by some one of his associates, of whom Luke, Barnabas, and Apollos are most prominently mentioned. JAMES and JUDE are either apostles or brethren of Christ, who were most intimately associated with the apostles.

55. Discussions bearing on the canonical authority of the different books of the Bible are akin to those which are to follow immediately upon the purity of the text. It is essential to know what

properly belongs to Sacred Scripture before we attempt to interpret it and accept the responsibility of incorporating the teachings of its several books into our systems of doctrinal belief. It is by no means an unimportant result of our investigations, that the apocryphal books of the Old Testament are found to be destitute of canonical authority. Had there been evidence that Christ and the apostles endorsed the Apocrypha as they did the canonical books of the Old Testament, the whole theology of Protestantism, like that of the Roman Catholic church, must have been adjusted to a belief in the intercession of angels and saints, and to a belief in purgatory and of the efficacy of prayers for the dead. The discussions concerning the few books in the Old Testament, about whose canonicity doubts have been expressed, are the less important, from the fact that those books contain no peculiar doctrines, but they belong rather to that portion of sacred literature designed to give a more vivid impression of some important phases of the truth. We accept them, however, even when we do not fully understand their purposes, as nevertheless organically connected with the Bible. They are not, like the Apocrypha, parasites, but are genuine branches of the tree.

Having determined that each of the books of the New Testament as it now stands properly forms a part of Sacred Scripture, and thereby having assumed the responsibility of incorporating their ethical and religious teaching into our systems of doctrine, we must next consider whether we have these books in their original and uncorrupted form.

VI.

INSPIRATION AND TEXTUAL CRITICISM.

56. THE inspiration of the writers who composed the Bible does not involve that of those who, at a later time, copied and translated the volume. Textual criticism is a science. By it we may ascertain, with a remarkable degree of accuracy, the form of our sacred literature as it came from the hands of the inspired writers, and as it was received and approved by the primitive churches. Those original writings are, so to speak, the geological formations deposited in the ages of inspiration, and which it is our business now reverently to study. When we find these deposits we find the rock. The secondary processes by which we ascertain the metes and bounds of this underlying solid stratum of the divine word, do not, indeed, lay claim to inspiration; but a marked divine providence is clearly visible in the provisions made for securing confidence in the conclusions arrived at through the processes of textual criticism.

57. The text of the New Testament to which we go for enlightenment is, in the main, established beyond all controversy. The grounds of this general confidence are so evident that they can be made plain even to popular apprehension.

Everything indicates that, during the generation succeeding the apostles, the writings received by the primitive churches as inspired must have been reproduced and disseminated with great rapidity and with a high degree of accuracy; for they emerge during the second century over a vast area and in many places, but with surprising agreement, not only in substance of thought, but in all important forms of expression, and even in minute particulars of style. In the second century (probably in the early part of it) nearly the whole of the New Testament, as we now have it, was translated into Syriac.[1] During the same period, in Northern Africa and Italy, translations appeared also in Latin. An Egyptian version also dates from the same period. The great writers of the latter part of the second century, and of the first half of the third century,— Justin Martyr (about 150), Irenæus (175), Clement of Alexandria (200), Tertullian (220), and Origen (220),— abound in quotations from the New Testament; so that we could almost reconstruct the volume from their treatises alone. A century or two later

[1] See paragraphs 45 and 45 *b*.

copies (still preserved) were made, presumably from the best accredited manuscripts then extant. Notable among these early copies are *first*, the CODEX SINAITICUS (now in the library of St. Petersburg), discovered by Tischendorf in 1859 in a convent on Mount Sinai, and dating, in all probability, from about A. D. 350; *second*, the CODEX VATICANUS (preserved in the Vatican library at Rome), and dating doubtless from about the same period with the Sinaiticus; *third*, the CODEX ALEXANDRINUS (brought from Constantinople to London in 1753), and dating about A. D. 450; *fourth*, CODEX EPHRAEMI (now in the library at Paris), and doubtless dating also from about the middle of the fifth century; *fifth*, CODEX BEZAE (now in Cambridge, England), and dating from the close of the fifth, or the first of the sixth, century of our era. Besides these there are more than fifteen hundred manuscripts of a later date. Thus it appears, as one of the highest authorities has said, that "Providence has ordered it so that the New Testament can appeal to a far larger number of all kinds of original sources than the whole of the rest of ancient Greek literature."[1]

58. As is to be expected in books made by hand, no two copies exactly agree. This does not, however, lead to the endless confusion which some might suppose, for in a multitude of manuscripts,

[1] Tischendorf, Introduction to New Testament, p. viii.

as in a multitude of counsellors, there is safety. The variations in one manuscript offset those in another; and out of the whole the original text emerges with a surprisingly small range of uncertainty. According to the latest and best authority, seven-eighths of the words of the New Testament have passed the ordeal of textual criticism without question; and of the remaining one-eighth, only a small fraction are subject to reasonable doubt; so that fifty-nine sixtieths of the words of the New Testament, as they came from the original authors, are known with practical certainty. And even of the one-sixtieth open to question the larger part of the doubt pertains to changes of order in the words, and other comparative trivialities; "so that the amount of what can in any sense be called substantial variation is but a small fraction of the whole residuary variation, and can hardly form more than a thousandth part of the entire text."[1]

59. As illustrative of the trivial character of the changes suggested by textual criticism, we will give a few specimens from the eighth edition of Tischendorf's Critical Greek Testament, which happens to be at hand. Opening at the first verse of the first chapter of Romans, the only critical question raised is whether to read "Jesus Christ" or "Christ Jesus"; which, as any one may see,

[1] Westcott and Hort's Introduction to the New Testament in Original Greek, p. 2.

has no bearing upon the meaning of the verse. The same question is raised about the order of these same words in a number of other places in this Epistle, and in each case goes to swell the list of textual variations.

On verse third one question is whether to spell D*aveid*, or D*avid*, or D*abid*. The second critical note upon this verse is whether, in the phrase "was born of the seed of David," the reading should be γενομένου or γεννωμένου, the second of which *must* mean "was born," and the first *may* mean "was born," but would admit of the more generic construction "was made"; so the change, if supported by sufficient evidence, would be of small account; but the evidence in favor of the common text is overwhelming, and it is therefore retained.

Upon verse fourth it is found that the word translated "declared" is, according to some authorities, compounded with a preposition (πρό), making it mean "declared *beforehand*." There is a variation, also, respecting the case of the word (πνεῦμα) meaning "spirit"; and some authorities would insert "and" before the prepositional clause "according to the spirit." None of these changes, however, is particularly important, and none is approved by any modern critic.

There are no other critical notes until reaching verse 7, where there is a question as to the retention of Ῥώμη in the passage, and as to whether the clause "beloved of God" should not be replaced by one meaning "in the love of God"; but the evidence for these changes is slight, and the received text stands.

In verse 8 some texts would omit an untranslated connective, which, if introduced, would be represented by our word "then," "First, then." There is also a question as to which of two synonymous prepositions (περί, ὑπέρ) should stand in the phrase translated "for you all." And so, for the most part, the dull process of textual criticism proceeds, — with only now and then an eventful episode touching a change which would in any serious manner affect the sense.

60. We would not, however, throw any discredit upon the work of the textual critics, but would give them their full share of praise for their infinite patience and untiring industry. The world owes them an unbounded debt of gratitude for their work. The Greek Text of the New Testament, by Westcott and Hort, represents the combined labor of two scholars for thirty years; and even so they were but working over material collected by other investigators who had devoted their whole lives to the examination of original authorities. But our remarks are designed to emphasize the fact that textual critics are not the ones who receive the impression that there is any such un-

certainty respecting the text of the New Testament as seriously to affect the doctrine of inspiration. There are, indeed, a number of important disputed readings, and a number of passages formerly received and depended upon as proof-texts which in the present light must be omitted, and a number of important readings that must be displaced by others better attested. The doubts, however, respecting some portions of the text are no more serious than the doubts which have always existed respecting the true interpretation of certain portions of Scripture; and, while some of the changes or omissions deprive us of proof-texts upon which we had been accustomed to depend, all these changes together will not seriously modify a single vital doctrine of the Bible.

61. Among the more important omissions and modifications of passages in the New Testament made necessary by modern textual criticism, the following may be mentioned by way of illustration: An important passage in determining the authorship of the Book of Hebrews depends for its force upon the presence or absence of a single iota (ι). If in Heb. x. 34 we read with the received text δεσμοῖς, instead of δεσμίοις with the modern critics, the passage should be translated "Ye had compassion of *me* in my bonds," which would plainly indicate that Paul was the writer; but if, with better authorities, we insert the additional iota (ι) we

must translate "Ye had compassion upon *them* that were in bonds,"—thus removing the verse altogether from the Pauline side of the argument. In 1 Tim. i. 4 the change of a single letter in a single Greek word transforms the clause "*godly edifying* which is in faith" into "*a dispensation of God* which is in faith" (οἰκοδομίαν changed to οἰκονομίαν). In 1 Tim. iii. 16 there has been a long-continued and heated controversy over the reading; some making the last clause read "*God* was manifest in the flesh," others, "he *who* was manifested in the flesh." The forms of the two Greek words upon which this reading depends (ΘC "God" and OC "who") are so nearly alike that they could readily be confounded in a badly worn manuscript.

At the behest of textual criticism, too, we must probably omit the doxology from the Lord's prayer in Matthew; and in the angelic annunciation of the Saviour's birth, instead of finding a general proclamation of "Peace and good will to men," we must read "Peace to men of good pleasure." In Matt. v. 22 we shall no longer read "angry with his brother *without a cause*," but simply "angry with his brother." The last eleven verses of Mark were probably not written by the same author as the rest of the book. It is a question just how much apostolic authority should be ascribed to the verses. John v. 4, which explains the disturbance of the water in the Pool of Bethesda by the theory that an angel went down at a certain time and troubled it, is omitted by the best texts. The oldest texts also omit the first eleven verses of John viii., containing the account of the woman taken in adultery; but this, like the last eleven verses of Mark, is too long to have been inserted by accident, and too striking in its character to have been admitted into the Scriptures at the early date at which we find it in some of the versions and quotations of the fathers, except on good authority. On the other hand, it has been affirmed, that as this passage in John occupies exactly four of the pages of the papyrus sheets upon which the Gospel was originally written, it may by a trifling accident have been easily omitted from the exemplar from which were copied the early manuscripts that want it (the Sinaitic, Alexandrian, and the Vatican). The loss of four of the fragile papyrus pages would not be an unlikely event; but their addition without overwhelming evidence would be most unlikely.[1]

But critics are all agreed that the clause in the seventh and eighth verses of the fifth chapter of First John, relating to the three that bear record in heaven, should be omitted, as it is found in no ancient manuscript, in no ancient version, and is quoted by none of the early fathers when arguing

---

[1] See monograph of J. Rendel Harris in the Supplement to the American Journal of Philology for Dec. 1882.

on the subject of the Trinity. God did not, however, leave that doctrine to the attestation of a single text; but the doctrine is so wrought into the warp and woof of the New Testament that a half dozen proof-texts might be removed without seriously diminishing its certainty.

62. These are sufficient to illustrate the character of the claims of textual criticism. We may profitably turn our attention to a few of the facts and principles from which this science justly derives its authority. As already mentioned, there are two manuscripts — the Sinaitic and the Vatican — which clearly antedate all others; and these are the two whose authority has come to have preponderating weight above that of almost any combination against them. It comes, therefore, to be an important and interesting question why we should pay such deference to these two manuscripts, which are themselves but copies made two hundred and fifty or three hundred years later than the originals. What is there to show that manuscripts of the sixth or seventh century were not copied either from the originals or from manuscripts executed earlier than the date of the Sinaitic or Vatican? The answer is, that by scientific reasoning we can prove the Sinaitic and Vatican manuscripts to be not only earlier in date than others, but also to be nearer the originals in form and structure. In arriving at this result we are

dependent upon two or three obvious rules of internal evidence.

63. In copying manuscripts, the changes which are likely to be made by an honest scribe (and there are no indications at all of dishonest attempts to manipulate the ancient texts upon which we most rely) are in the direction, *first*, of removing seeming grammatical errors; and *second*, of adding explanatory words in difficult passages for the sake of removing apparent obscurity; and *third*, where parallel records like the Gospels occur, of assimilating one to the other. Little more than the mere statement of these principles is needed to carry conviction. We all know how natural it is to add a word which logically completes the idea expressed. Few persons, in repeating the promise of the Saviour to be with us where two or three are gathered together,[1] would limit themselves to the exact words of Scripture, but would very naturally make that addition [2] so often heard, and which so perfectly completes the idea implicitly contained in the passage, and would say, "For where two or three are gathered together in my name, there am I in the midst of them, *and that to bless.*" The true reading in Matt. xxv. 6 doubtless is, "Behold, the bridegroom"; but a respectable number of texts read, "Behold, the bridegroom *cometh.*" In this case nothing new is really added,

---

[1] **Matt. xviii. 20.** [2] Printed in italics below.

but the fuller form merely states *ex*plicitly the *im*plicit contents of the shorter form. Again, in Matt. xviii. 28 the older manuscripts read, "Pay what thou owest," while the later manuscripts read, "Pay *me* what thou owest." So in Luke xxiv. 53 the older manuscripts read, "were continually in the temple, blessing God"; while the later manuscripts read, "were continually in the temple, *praising* and blessing God." As any one can see, this instinctive and unconscious tendency to round out the expression of the idea conveyed, is a force which would be constantly operating upon the minds of scribes, and would tend to corrupt the text. Furthermore, this tendency would be still more strongly felt when, as in the case of the parallel passages found in the first three Gospels, one form was originally fuller than another. Familiarity with the longer form of one evangelist would render it a most natural occurrence for the scribe in writing the shorter form of one evangelist, to fill it out according to the longer form of the other, and thus assimilate the two. For example, in Matt. viii. 33 we read that the keepers of the swine that were possessed, "fled, and went their ways into the city, and told." In Luke[1] the older texts read simply, they "fled, and told" it. Very naturally, however, later scribes, familiar with the form in Matthew, filled out the statement in Luke

[1] Luke viii. 34.

so that it should read, as in the later texts, the keepers "fled, and went, and told"; thus unconsciously assimilating the two accounts. So, again, in Mark i. 2 the older manuscripts give an abbreviated quotation from Malachi, "Behold, I send my messenger before thy face, who shall prepare thy way."[1] In Matt. xi. 10 and Luke vii. 27 the quotation is rounded out by the addition of "before thee," making it read, "shall prepare thy way *before thee.*" Hence, some later scribe naturally, and perhaps unconsciously, filled out the quotation in Mark, so as to assimilate it in form to that with which all were familiar in the other Gospels.

64. A third unconscious force operating to secure slight variations in the text, consists in the tendency, always present in the scribe, to remove seeming obscurities and grammatical blunders, which he supposes may have come into the text through the carelessness of a former scribe.

In estimating the force of these unconscious tendencies operating upon the minds of scribes, we are not permitted to restrict ourselves to single instances, but are bound to examine a great number of cases, so as to obtain by the law of *general average* a conclusion that is substantial. Such a survey of the facts proves, beyond all reasonable doubt, that the two oldest manuscripts — the Sinaitic and Vatican — are not only the oldest

[1] Mal. iii. 1.

manuscripts, but are, by all odds, the most correct manuscripts of the New Testament in existence; so that the presumption is well-nigh overwhelming that the readings in which they agree are closest to the original copies. The general correctness of these manuscripts is shown *a*. by their relative freedom from the errors naturally arising from the three causes just mentioned; *b*. from the confirmation which their readings in general derive from the oldest versions; and *c*. from the quotations of the early fathers. We will illustrate by a single case occurring in Mark i. 11, where the Sinaitic and Vatican texts read, "in *thee* I am well pleased," but the later texts give it, "in *whom* I am well pleased," which is also the reading in the corresponding passage in Matt. iii. 17. The text in Matthew is unquestionably "in whom"; that in Mark only is open to dispute.

Now, on the principle of assimilation, in Mark the change from *in thee* to *in whom* would be most naturally effected by a scribe who remembered the form in Matthew. As we have said, the probability in this single case that an error has arisen from assimilation would be slight; but when we find that, as the best of authorities assure us, and as any one can see by a few hours' examination, the instances of probable error naturally arising from assimilation are fifty times more numerous in the later manuscripts than in the Sinaitic and

Vatican, these two earlier manuscripts come to have great independent authority, and on this ground alone we should give the preference to the reading in Mark, "in *thee* I am well pleased." But this is not all. The reading "in thee" is independently proved to be very old from its incorporation into the earliest versions, namely, the Syriac, the Latin, and the Egyptian. And here again, the coincidence of the oldest versions with the reading of the Sinaitic and the Vatican manuscripts would be of slight account if it existed only in this single instance. But the coincidences are sufficiently frequent to prove the law. Tregelles, one of the highest authorities upon the subject, estimates that the instances in which these old texts are proved by the versions to contain the oldest known readings number between two and three thousand; and thus they are shown by an independent process not only to be old themselves, but to represent most closely the text which is the oldest.

Again, the Sinaitic and the Vatican, and the allied cluster of manuscripts which they represent, are proved to contain the very oldest readings by comparing them with the numerous quotations from Scripture found in the writings of the church fathers of the second and third centuries.

65. There can be no question that modern

textual criticism is a science, resting upon a solid basis of observation and natural law. If we could be as confident that we are correct in interpreting Scripture as we are in fixing upon the original text, we might count ourselves fortunate indeed. It would, however, be too much to hope by application of the rules of textual criticism to remove every obscurity relating to the original copies; but these obscurities may certainly be reduced to very insignificant proportions, so as to be of little more account than the spots upon the sun.

Having, therefore, by these scientific critical processes confirmed our confidence in the general accuracy of the Greek text of the sacred writings, and having eliminated the few corruptions that had unconsciously been incorporated into these writings, the next question in order will be, What do the Scriptures mean? for, as before remarked, it is the sense of the word of God which has authority, and not the sound.

VII.

INTERPRETATION OF SCRIPTURE.

66. Many erroneous opinions concerning the Bible obtain popular credence from want of familiarity with the principles and results of biblical interpretation. Biblical interpretation is a science with well-established principles of procedure, and whose conclusions are by no means so indefinite and uncertain as is frequently represented. The province of this science is to ascertain the meaning of the Bible. The doctrine of the infallibility of the Bible has suffered much from lack of accurate definition, and most of the objections urged against it disappear upon making the discriminations which the nature of the subject demands. Infallibility can be attributed to the Bible only as a whole, and as related to its designed effect in human history. Much of the fallibility attributed to it belongs to its interpreters, and arises from their needless ignorance and prejudice. The doctrine of inspiration implies that, as a divine factor in human history, the Bible is perfectly adapted to its work. That work, however, is much more comprehensive than some of the commentators and critics are willing to admit. An historical revelation of the nature, character, and purposes of God must of necessity be many-sided, or it would not be adapted to the varying conditions of the human race. It must meet the wants of the ages to which it is first given, and at the same time be couched in such language and presented in such form that future ages shall be able to extract its meaning. The written word of God must have points of attachment adapting it to use among rude and barbarous tribes,[1] and at the same time must be so full of meaning, so perfect in its form, and so sublime in its outlook, as to satisfy the wants of the most cultivated ages. In the same storehouse we must find both milk for babes and meat for strong men. The truth must be preserved in such plain precepts and bold outlines as shall justify the assertion that "wayfaring men, though fools, shall not err therein."[2] At the same time revelation must lead on from glory to glory, and securely and wisely conduct the race forward toward the ever-widening horizon of eternity.

67. Reverence is one of the first duties imposed upon man by the presence of a divine revelation. A divine revelation is in its very nature calculated to overawe the human mind. And if we really believe that God is speaking to us through

---

[1] See below, chapter ix.   [2] Isa. xxxv. 8.

the Bible, we shall, like Moses at the burning bush, put off our shoes from our feet,[1] and bow our heads in subdued reverence to hear the message which that voice brings. For various reasons it is impossible for one who believes in the divine authenticity of Christianity to treat the Bible as he would other books. In our interpretation of the Bible we are not at liberty to overlook the divine element pervading it. To interpret the Bible as if the writers had no more authority than comes from the ordinary illumination of the Holy Spirit, is to ignore the most prominent teachings of the whole volume.

68. The written word of God, like the Word which became flesh, must needs be human in its manward aspect; for the written word is divine thought manifest in human *language* as Christ was God manifest in human *flesh*. As the compound personality of Christ was conditioned by the flesh, so the compound character of a written revelation is conditioned by the nature of language. As God in becoming incarnate did not take upon him the form of angels, but of the seed of Abraham, so the written revelation is not sent in a form adapted to heavenly beings, but in a form suited to men. And it is in this that the perfection of the word of God consists. It *is* adapted to men. Though a veritable deposit of divine thought, the Bible is

[1] Ex. iii. 5.

provided with all the allurements necessary to attract men to search for its divine message; and when found the message is accompanied with all the appropriate indications of its divine character. It goes, therefore, for little as against the doctrine of inspiration to say that in subjecting the divine word to a written form it is thereby made dependent on human language, which is variously imperfect. Of course a written revelation is thus dependent, and for that very reason its writers needed the special supervision of the Divine Spirit. Nor does it weigh against the divine authority of the Scriptures, that a written revelation must take color from the mental and moral conditions of the age in which it was first made, and be affected by the mental and moral condition of the individual human authors; for these are phenomenal elements whose relation to the central cause can be easily ascertained. It is the province of the science of interpretation, by a careful survey of the whole field, to eliminate the influence of these superficial elements, and penetrate to the region of pure white light produced by a divine combination of complementary colors. It is a prime excellence of the Bible, that its thought is not contained solely in single forms of expression, but is discerned as a compound resultant of various forms. In "divers portions and in divers manners"[1] God has spoken

[1] Heb. i. 1.

to the world through holy men and prophets; but all unite to produce a harmonious impression, and to secure the designed result.

69. An essential requisite to the proper interpretation of the Bible is a profound sense of human ignorance; hence the importance of the maxim, *Interpret the Bible with prayerfulness and sobriety.* Our knowledge is infinitesimal as compared with God's knowledge. This fact imposes humility upon the interpreter alike of God's work and of God's word. The outlying field of mystery — connected both with the clearly revealed facts of nature and of the Bible — must be allowed neither to discredit the facts we have nor to lead us into the fields of vague and useless speculation. A thousand questions can be asked concerning any plain matter of fact where one can be answered. In this respect nature and the Bible are alike; but nature is far more abundant in things to which we ascribe no definite design than the Bible is in facts in which we fail to see definite marks of inspiration. It is nevertheless true that in nature we can confidently attribute design to the sparrow's fall, and this not because we can definitely trace the design, but because the event is connected with a system which we have the best of reasons for believing is as a whole the product of design; and we can defy any one to prove the absence of purpose even in the minutest fact of nature. Thus, also, the inter-

preter of the Bible may freely acknowledge his ignorance concerning the precise function or meaning of many portions of Scripture, while holding, nevertheless, with the utmost confidence to the conviction that the Bible in every part *has* a divinely chosen function and significance. Where so much is clear, and the whole is so perspicuous, it devolves upon those who criticise the Bible in its minute details, to prove that the portions to which they object cannot possibly have any proper function in a divine revelation. We need not say that to prove such a universal negative is not an easy task. To succeed in the undertaking, the critic must be able to survey the whole universe, and to comprehend the wants of the human race in every detail.

70. Correlated with the previous principle, which puts in the foreground the necessary limitations of human knowledge, is another of a positive character, which may be stated as follows: *The more obscure portions of the Bible should be interpreted according to the evident main purpose of the whole;* or, in other words, we should assume that the Bible is consistent in itself; — hence, in interpreting it we must consider the relations of one part to another, and should take the clearer portions for our guide, while reverently attempting to discover the meaning of the obscurer parts.

71. Closely connected with the foregoing is the

principle that *the writers of the Bible are their own best expounders.* It is the more important to insist upon this principle since it is just now the object of so many attacks. One of the most impressive lines of evidence in proof of a pervasive divine element in the Bible consists in the remarkable unity binding it together from Genesis to Revelation. Though a collection of books most diverse in form and human authorship, there is a sublime strain of supernaturalism running through it all, and separating it by a sharp line of demarcation from all other literature. It is necessary for the biblical interpreter constantly to keep in view this assumed and asserted element of the supernatural in the Bible, or he will fail of comprehending even its simplest passages. It is this pervasive supernatural element that gives to the Old Testament its dignity, and to the writers of the New their consistency. Without it the writings of Christ and the apostles must fail to command and retain our respect. There are divinely chosen words of prophecy in the Old Testament telling of Christ that should come. There are types in the Old Testament which can be fully understood only as seen in the light reflected back upon them from the New Testament. We cannot divorce the Old Testament from the New without destroying the authority and meaning of both. The Old Testament is not perfect without the New, and the

New Testament is incomprehensible without the Old.

72. We do not see how some recent writers can maintain the respect which they profess to do for the authors of the New Testament while speaking so contemptuously of their ability to interpret the Old Testament. For example, we find Professor Toy saying, when speaking of Paul's method of interpretation, that "where he has a thesis to establish from the Old Testament (especially in Galatians and Romans), he employs without stint the forced and spiritualizing interpretation of the times. . . . Paul's methodical exposition (see Rom. iv. and Gal. iii., iv.) was probably taken from the school-teaching of the Jerusalem doctors; he and they were forced, by the necessities of a long-drawn-out argument, into a thoroughly arbitrary style of exegesis."[1] The dogmatic material of the Book of Hebrews "differs from that of Paul; . . . but its hermeneutical method, like his, is rabbinical. . . . Its lofty and inspiring religious thought is violently connected with the Old Testament by an unsound exegesis."[2] Even Professor Ladd can say: "It is this keen hunt for ethico-religious truth, as it exists in its essential unity under various forms of expression, which induces some of the quotations from the Old

---

[1] Quotations of the New Testament, p. xxxvi.
[2] Ibid., p. xxxvii.

Testament in the New that are most difficult and even impossible critically to justify."[1] And Professor Toy can describe the rabbinical exegesis of Christ's day as utterly unhistorical, unscientific, arbitrary, "uncontrolled by sound principles of interpretation";[2] ready, on the one hand, to invest each word of Scripture "with an independent meaning, which it retained even when wrested from its proper position in the discourse"; and, on the other hand, to regard each sentence or word as "a mysterious sign of such ideas as the devout, but undirected, imagination of the reader demanded"; and yet say "the New Testament method is the same in general as this," "only far more cautious and reserved." Again, Professor Toy affirms that the Old Testament is to be made its own interpreter.[3] "This fulfilment [of the Old Testament promises] is brought out in the New Testament, though in most cases by, or in connection with, a method of interpretation that cannot be called legitimate. The natural, historical interpretation seeming to them not to yield satisfactory results, the New Testament writers spiritualize; but faulty exegesis is no great matter alongside of the power of their theme, and the inspiration of their pure and strong spiritual thought."[4]

---

[1] Doctrine of Sacred Scripture, Vol. I. p. 172.
[2] Quotations of the New Testament, pp. xxii., xxiii.
[3] Ibid., p. xxvi.   [4] Ibid., p. xxvii.

73. We cannot, however, admit that it is in accordance with the best canons of hermeneutical science, as applied to the Old Testament, to reckon the words of Jesus and the apostles as of no authority in interpreting the Old Testament. We trust few would be willing to accept the statement of Professor Toy, that, "as an individual man he [Jesus] had of necessity a definite, restricted intellectual outfit and outlook; and these could be only those of his day and generation."[1] It by no means follows, as Professor Toy asserts, that because Jesus as a man does not know the day of consummation,[2] he may not be supposed to know the science of the criticism of the Old Testament. Such a use of the word science is, to say the least, far from being felicitous. For what is the science of any given subject if it be not a methodical summary of what we know about the subject? and what shall we think of Christ and the apostles, if they pretended to expound the Old Testament, and did not know how to do it, and did not understand what the Old Testament was intended to teach? Instead of saying, then, with Professor Toy, that it was clearly not the purpose of the New Testament writers to teach exegesis,[3] we should say, that to unfold the meaning of the Old Testament was exactly what they professed to do. And,

---

[1] Quotations of the New Testament, p. xxviii.
[2] Matt. xxiv. 36.   [3] Ibid., p. xxx.

in unfolding that teaching, Christ and the apostles bring clearly to light a supernatural harmony between the writings of the Old Testament and the facts and doctrines of the New. It therefore certainly is a most important exegetical principle that our investigations regarding any part of the Scripture should be guided by the interpretation put upon it in other portions of Scripture.

We especially need this loyalty to the writers of the New Testament, not only to obtain that view of the typical character of much of the Old Testament which is necessary to justify its application to the facts of the New Testament; but we need to adhere to the New Testament models of interpretation, in order to restrain us from the unlicensed use of type and allegory.

74. For example, in Matt. xxii. 43 the one hundred and tenth Psalm, which begins, "The Lord said unto my Lord, Sit thou at my right hand," and in verse 4 says, "Thou *art* a priest forever after the order of Melchizedek," is interpreted as referring to Christ himself. These words, Christ says, were spoken by David in the Spirit (ἐν πνεύματι). The importance of the application may be inferred from its reappearing in the parallel passages in Mark[1] and Luke,[2] and, again, in Peter's sermon on the day of Pentecost,[3] as well as in Heb. i. 13. Thus the extended allegory in

---

[1] Mark xii. 36.   [2] Luke xx. 42.   [3] Acts ii. 34, 35.

Hebrews concerning Melchizedek and Christ draws its warrant from the Saviour's own interpretation of Ps. cx. In Matt. xxvi. 31 Christ applies to himself the words of Zech. xiii. 7, "I will smite the shepherd, and the sheep of the flock shall be scattered." In Luke iv. 18, 19 ([18] "The Spirit of the Lord is upon me, because he anointed me to preach good tidings to the poor: he hath sent me to proclaim release to the captives, and recovering of sight to the blind, to set at liberty them that are bruised, [19] to proclaim the acceptable year of the Lord") Christ applies to himself the words of Isaiah.[1] In Luke xxii. 37, Christ says of the words, "And he was reckoned with transgressors" (taken from Isa. liii. 12), "This which is written must be fulfilled in me."

In the last three passages Christ clearly gives his own sanction to a profounder and more far-reaching interpretation of the prophecies than appears on their face. The true idea is that all the offices under the theocracy were typical of Christ. Christ combines all in one. He is priest in the absolute sense, and a real king. In Matt. xxvi. 31, as well as in the tenth chapter of John, Christ calls himself the "shepherd." Again, in Matt. xxiv. 15 Christ interprets Dan. ix. 27; xi. 31; xii. 11, as referring to what was about to occur in the destruction of Jerusalem by the

---

[1] Isa. lxi. 1, 2; lviii. 6; xxix. 18.

Romans.[1] Or if "the abomination of desolation" be referred to the profanation of the temple by Antiochus Epiphanes, the occurrences under Titus would be an event of the same class prefigured by that. Christ has also, in emphatic and numerous ways, given his consent to the idea that the types of the Old Testament refer to him and his times.[2] In Mark ix. 13 Elijah is said to be a type of John the Baptist. We are thus led to suppose that the similarity between these men — both in their character and their history — was ordered by Divine Providence. Nor is it unusual for Christ to refer in general terms to the whole Old Testament as a prophecy of himself.[3] The only quotation of Christ which seems even to savor of rabbinical sophistry is in Matt. xxii. 32, where he proves the possibility of the resurrection from Ex. iii. 6, "I am the God of Abraham," etc., and adds, "God is not the God of the *dead*, but of the *living*." The force of his argument, however, does not lie in the use of the present tense (I am), — for the verb is not expressed at all in the Hebrew of the original passage, — but in the inevitable in-

---

[1] See Cowles on Dan. ix. 26, 27.

[2] See John v. 39, 46; vii. 38; where the Scriptures and Moses are said to have written of him. Cf. John iii. 14, "As Moses lifted up the serpent," etc., and the passages referring to the Lord's supper.

[3] See Matt. xxvi. 24, 54, 56; Luke xxiv. 27, 44; John xiii. 18; xvii. 12.

ference that when God pays so much attention to creatures as he did to the patriarchs, and calls himself their God, they must be more than mere transient existences, or there is a striking incongruity in the amount of attention paid to them. With such a view of the passage there is no tinge of sophistry in it.

We conclude, then, that Christ has given his sanction to the view expressed by De Wette; viz. that "the whole Old Testament is one great prophecy, one great type, of him who was to come, and is come; and that the typological comparison of the Old Testament with the New is no mere idle play; and it cannot be pure accident that the evangelical history in most important particulars runs parallel with the Mosaic."[1]

75. Paul likewise interprets the Old Testament in a typical sense. The most striking example is Gal. iv. 21-31, which the apostle in verse 24 calls an allegory. Hagar and her descendants symbolize the law given on Mount Sinai and its adherents; while Sarah and her descendants correspond to the church of Christ. Again, Isa. liv. 1 is applied[2] to the enlargement of the Jewish church which took place upon the introduction of the Gentiles into the Christian church. Gen. xxi. 10 is likewise applied[3] to the Jews, who were

---

[1] Cf. the author's Logic of Christian Evidences, pp. 270-274.
[2] Gal. iv. 27.   [3] Gal. iv. 30.

rejected because of their unreasonable attachment to the law.

The quotation of Deut. xxv. 4 in 1 Cor. ix. 9, 10; and 1 Tim. v. 18 illustrates in an admirable way the true method of bringing out the deeper spiritual sense of the Scriptures. In Timothy the inference is unexpressed, but inevitable. The Scripture saith, Thou shalt not muzzle the ox when he treadeth out the corn; the inference is, *much less* should you withhold temporal support from spiritual teachers. A universal principle appears in a special application. But in 1 Cor. ix. 9, 10 the apostle seems to say that the original passage had no literal meaning, and that God did not care for oxen; that this was said *altogether* (πάντως) on our account. This may be explained as an hyperbole. The Old Testament familiarized us with the principle involved in our treatment of animals, but its broader application was of such *superlative* importance that it completely overshadows the other. Here, too, the correspondence between type and antitype is looked upon as designed.

In 1 Cor. x. 1–4 the pillar of fire, the manna, and the living water of Moses' time, are spoken of as designed types of Christ. In the fourth and sixth chapters of John the last two of these same types are used.

In Gal. iii. 16 the argument seems to turn on

the realistic idea of species (σπέρμα). The interpretation here has certainly brought out hidden meaning in the argument. There was a pre-established harmony between the physical element giving unity to a species and the spiritual element giving unity to believers in Christ.

Both in Hebrew and Greek as well as in English the word for "seed" has a different meaning in the singular from that conveyed by the plural. In the singular the specific character of the seed is thrown into the foreground, in the plural the individual. Mustard *seed* has a very different shade of meaning from mustard *seeds*. So the seed of Abraham is only one in kind, and in a very real sense it is Christ, who, in becoming head of that seed, imparts specific character and unity to it.

The ninth chapter of Romans well shows the ordinary historical method of Paul's quotations. The allegory of Hagar in Gal. iv. 27 is virtually repeated here. There is an Israel of the flesh and an Israel of faith.[1] This last verse, "I lay in Zion a stone of stumbling," is applied to Christ in a typical sense.[2]

Acts xiii. 35 is interesting as giving a Messianic interpretation to Ps. xvi. 10, which could not be

---

[1] See quotations in verses 8, 9, 12, 13, 15, 17, 25, 29, 33.

[2] See further Gal. iii. 8; Rom. iv. 11, 17, in all of which places an enlarged meaning is given to an historical parallel. It is the true principle of evolution in the history of the church.

drawn except on the view that Christ is the person in whom all Old Testament types and history centre and receive their fulfilment. Many of Paul's citations would seem *mere* accommodations but for this view of the typical character of all the Old Testament literature. The original sense of the passages quoted is often restricted or enlarged by the apostle, but never falsified. "The apostle proceeds like one who, having seen a completed picture and then cast a glance upon the outline sketch, believes he sees more indicated there than he who is familiar only with the sketch."[1] At the same time, Paul reflects to some extent the influence of his rabbinical training. This, however, instead of *dis*crediting Paul, should really *ac*credit some elements of the rabbinical method of interpretation, and prove that there was a measure of truth in that method.

76. In the Gospels (especially in Matthew and John) the words of prophecy are usually applied with the distinct statement that this or that event took place "in order that it might be fulfilled [ἵνα πληρωθῇ, *hina plerothee*]."[2] In many of these cases the alleged purposes seem insignificant and incidental. For example, in Matt. ii. 15 the object of Christ's journey to Egypt is said to be "that it

---

[1] Tholuck in *Bibliotheca Sacra*, Vol. xi. p. 597.
[2] Matt. i. 22; ii. 15; iv. 14; xxi. 4; Mark xiv. 49; John xii. 38; xiii. 18; xix. 24, 28, 36.

might be fulfilled which was spoken by the Lord through the prophet, saying, Out of Egypt did I call my Son."[1] In Matt. ii. 23 Christ's abode in Nazareth is said to have occurred "that it might be fulfilled which was spoken by the prophets, that he should be called a Nazarene." This merely expresses the idea conveyed in Isa. iv. 2; xi. 1; Jer. xxiii. 5; Zech. iii. 8; vi. 12, especially Isa. xi. 1, "There shall come forth a rod out of the stem of Jesse, and a Branch" (נֵצֶר *netzer*). Nazareth derives its name from the same root. The name of the place was expressive of the conditions of Christ.[2] But in Zechariah a different word (צֶמַח, *tsemach*) is translated "branch." The question is, Did these occurrences take place on purpose to fulfil the words of the prophet, or, as in Matt. ii. 23, are the words chosen in part to round out a paronomasia? The most satisfactory answer is, That from the divine point of view the full design or final cause of an event is never a single use to which it is put, but the sum of all the uses to which it is ever put. The incidental advantages of a plan are a part of its warrant. The many and minute parallelisms between the Old Testament and the history of Christ were, we may believe, designed for the sake of the evidence they furnish to the supernatural character of the revelation. We need not hesitate, then, in giving ἵνα, *hina*

---

[1] Hosea xi. 1.   [2] See John i. 46.

(in order that), its natural sense as expressing a purpose. God purposed the salvation of the world through these means. These means were correlated to the future demands of men for evidence. On the other hand, there can be no question that the Greek word ἵνα, *hina*, had in New Testament times lost much of its old purposive force, and is often to be translated *so that*, instead of *in order that;* as, for example, in John ix. 2, where the question is asked, "Who did sin, this man, or his parents, that [*hina*] he should be born blind?" Here it is clear that the speakers did not mean to say that the *design* of the sin was to produce blindness, but simply that the blindness was the *result* of sin. From attention to this usage of the word *hina* many of the difficulties connected with the use of this formula disappear. But, as just remarked, the difficulties are really not so serious as is often alleged. The fulfilment of prophecy is multifarious, and the speaker who alleges a fulfilment in a particular case does not necessarily assert that the whole intent of the prophecy was limited to that particular event.

Matt. i. 22, 23, from Isa. vii. 14, presents more difficulties than almost any other quotation. The occurrence of the word παρθένος, *parthenos* (virgin), in Matthew, and in the Septuagint of Isaiah, shows that the evangelist regards the quotation as a true prophecy; yet verses 15 and 16 seem to show that the prophecy was spoken of some virgin then living and of a fulfilment in the immediate future. The probable explanation is that which regards the person in whom the prophecy was immediately fulfilled as a type of Christ. This he was in many ways, especially in his relation to those times of depression.[1]

John xii. 15 (Zech. ix. 9) was a remarkable symbolic occurrence. The Old Testament taught Israel to expect a king. The genealogical tables show that Christ was the rightful heir to David's throne. On the occasion referred to he was now hailed as king, but was mounted not upon a horse, which was an emblem of war,[2] but upon an ass, which was the animal usually ridden in times of peace.

But we need not multiply instances. Christ, Paul, and the evangelists agree in regarding the Old Testament as the fruitful soil in which the New has its roots; but the fruit has a value far above that of the chemical elements of which it is composed. The Old Testament and the New form an organic whole, whose chief value consists in the combination and adjustment of the elementary parts.

77. At first sight three of the quotations in

---

[1] But see Fairbairn's Hermeneutical Manual, p. 456.
[2] See Hosea xiv. 3; Prov. xxi. 31; Jer. xvii. 25.

Hebrews seem without warrant in their application; viz. i. 6, 10–12; ii. 13.

a. Heb. i. 6 is from Ps. xcvii. 7. One would not infer from the Psalm that it had a Messianic import. It is addressed to Jehovah; and all the gods, *elohim* (אֱלֹהִים), are called upon to worship him. Here, as in some other places, אֱלֹהִים is translated by the Septuagint "angels," and this version is followed by the writer. This translation of *elohim* by "angels" occurs several times in the Septuagint.[1] Πάλιν (again) in this verse is also hard to explain, unless one holds to an introduction of Christ into the world before the incarnation.

b. Heb. i. 10–12 introduces Ps. cii. 25-27 as said of the Son; but in the original there is no intimation whatever of such an application.

c. Heb. ii. 13 is from 2 Sam. xxii. 3 and Isa. viii. 17, 18. Here the prophet seems to be the speaker. It certainly is only by introducing the typical sense that it can be applied to Christ.

In general, we may say of the application of the Old Testament quotations to Christ in the first two chapters of Hebrews, that they must reflect the view prevailing in the apostolic church concerning the exalted dignity of Christ's nature. The writer confidently assumes that these applications will be accepted by his readers. In Heb. i. 8, 9 ("But

[1] See Job xx. 15; Ps. viii. 5 (quoted in Heb. ii. 7); xcvi. 5; [English Bible xcvii. 7] cxxxviii. 1.

of the Son *he saith*, Thy throne, O God, is for ever and ever; and the sceptre of uprightness is the sceptre of thy kingdom. Thou hast loved righteousness, and hated iniquity; therefore God, thy God, hath anointed thee with the oil of gladness above thy fellows") the application of Ps. xlv. 6, 7 to Christ is in accordance with the Jewish interpretation of the passage. The first verse could be applied to the king only in a typical sense; and yet kings were called "gods" because of their official position. In Heb. i. 13 the Messianic application of Ps. cx. 1 is clear and natural; so also in Heb. vii. 17 the Messianic reference of Ps. cx. 4 is striking and appropriate if the typical view of prophecy be maintained. Even the names of Melchizedek and Salem are made to contain a prophecy;[1] as is also the omission in Genesis to give Melchizedek's genealogy. In the eleventh chapter of Hebrews the whole history of Israel is made symbolic.[2] In Heb. iv. 3–5, 9, 10, from Ps. xcv. 11, the Sabbath is made typical of God's eternal rest to which Israel is invited.

We cannot resist the conclusion that the writer's mode of interpreting all these Old Testament passages indicates the views of the apostolic church regarding inspiration. Altogether, the Book of

---

[1] Heb. vii. 2, 3.

[2] See verses 9, 10 (dwelling in tents); verses 13–16 (strangers and pilgrims).

Hebrews is a fitting development and consummation of the apostolic views foreshadowed and partially developed, *first*, by Christ; *second*, by Paul; *third*, by the evangelists, concerning the Old Testament as typical throughout of the new dispensation. The relation of these Testaments cannot be accidental. The harmony is too profound to have been produced by designing men as an afterthought. The Old Testament history and literature had a fulness of meaning that could have been impressed upon it only by divine design. Its true explanation and interpretation are found only in the New.

78. This pregnant character of much of the language of Scripture serves both to confirm the theory of the inspiration of the Bible and to relieve the theory from many apparent objections. The human architects of the Old Testament often builded better than they knew, as Caiaphas, the high-priest,[1] in saying that it was expedient "that one man should die for the people, and that the whole nation perish not," was the unwitting author of a prophecy. Clearly, also, it was not the object of Christ to make everything as plain as A B C. He evidently aimed to arouse the curiosity of his hearers; and, while bringing truth within their reach, still kept it so far out of sight that it should be obtained only as the reward of honest purpose

[1] John xi. 50.

and diligent search. He everywhere recognized the moral freedom of his hearers and the dependence of their intellectual attainments upon self-exertion. Thus in God's revelation in the Bible, as well as in nature, we find due recognition of the fact that the search after truth has as real value as the truth itself, and that the value of the truth lies in no small degree in the stimulus it supplies to men to search for it. It is on this principle that Christ spoke in parables,[1] "because seeing they see not, and hearing they hear not, neither do they understand."

Another reason for this mode of speech is that no divine truth in its fulness can be instantaneously revealed. Our powers of apprehension are limited, and we cannot grasp all truth at once. We see in part and understand in part. Our apprehensions of divine truth may be correct without being exhaustive. We may *find* God without *finding him out*. For example, many words of Christ were at first imperfectly understood by his disciples. They became clear only as seen in the light of subsequent events. "Destroy this temple, and in three days I will raise it up,"[2] had a deeper meaning than that attributed to it by his hearers. "And I, if I be lifted up from the earth, will draw all men unto myself,"[3] has fuller significance to us of this generation than to those of any previous age.

[1] Matt. xiii. 13.   [2] John ii. 19.   [3] John xii. 32.

Every missionary conquest is increasing the certainty and enlarging the fulness of the glorious promise. The prophecy of the destruction of Jerusalem in Matt. xvi. and xxiv. is so projected upon the background of the great judgment-day as to give a foreshortened view of all God's judgments from the time the words were uttered to the consummation of all things; and these prophecies of the second coming of Christ are connected with such admonitions[1] that the fanaticisms so often connected with their interpretation have been needless, except as they were providentially useful in enforcing upon later generations the duty of caution and humility in the interpretation of divine language.

This recognition by Christ of types and prophecies and pregnant utterances in the Old Testament is not only indispensable to the discernment of that fulness of meaning and sublimity of thought necessary to give consistency to the whole scheme of salvation, but is important as setting limits to our own tendency to employ typical and allegorical and spiritualizing methods of interpretation. Where Christ and the apostles have found a type, or an allegory, or a pregnant construction in the Old Testament, we may follow them with confidence; but beyond the limits set by their example in the use of these modes of

[1] Matt. xxiv.

interpretation it becomes us to proceed with caution.

The same is true concerning parables. Christ employed parables for instruction with the greatest of success. But it was because he spoke with *authority*. It is a significant fact that no one else has ever been able to add to the stock of human knowledge while speaking in parables. The use of parables implies a subtle correspondence between the works of God in nature and his works in grace; but the correspondence is so subtle that no one but He who spake as never man spake, has ever entered the field alone without becoming entangled in the mazes of profitless speculation and fantasy. It were well for the church if, in interpreting parables, her teachers had more nearly accepted the expositions of Christ himself as their models.

79. Another example illustrating the importance of interpreting Scripture by Scripture, is of too much moment to pass unnoticed. In 1 Thess. iv. 15, 17 Paul is understood by a large number of modern commentators as saying, that he himself expected to be alive at Christ's second coming to judge the world, and this is represented as an argument against the perfect trustworthiness of apostolic teachings. The words upon which this allegation is based are as follows: [15] " For this we say unto you by the word of the Lord, that we

that are alive, that are left unto the coming of the Lord, shall in no wise precede them that are fallen asleep. . . . (17) then we that are alive, that are left, shall together with them be caught up in the clouds, to meet the Lord in the air: and so shall we ever be with the Lord." The opinion that Paul expected to witness the end of the world and the resurrection before he died, is based on the clause reading, "We that are alive, that are left unto the coming of the Lord," where, at the first glance, one would say that Paul, by classing himself with those that are left, definitely expected that the resurrection would occur during his lifetime. Again, in Phil. iv. 5, it is said that "the Lord is at hand," and, in 1 Peter iv. 7, that "the end of all things is at hand"; while in 1 Cor. xv. 51, the apostle uses the first person plural, and seems again to class himself with those who shall not sleep, but shall be changed at the last trump. It cannot be denied, also, that in the early church there was a widespread expectation of "the speedy return of Christ." This expectation, however, was based not merely on the words of apostles, but on the reported language of Christ himself.[1]

It should be noted that the strictures just referred to bear not merely against the authority of Paul, but against the authority of Christ himself as reported by the evangelists. The appear-

[1] Matt. xvi. 28 and parallel passages; xxiv. 34; John xxi. 22.

ance of error, however, disappears when the whole field is surveyed, and the sacred writers are allowed to interpret themselves. Some principles checking and guiding us in the interpretation of their words, will be duly illustrated in future remarks upon the necessary brevity of Scripture[1] giving rise to apparent discrepancies in the narrative; and upon the freedom of expression allowable in transferring the thought of the Old Testament into the words of the New; and, indeed, are apparent in what has just now been said respecting the pregnant meaning frequently belonging to the facts and words employed in divine revelation. That these principles are applicable here is evident enough from the nature of the case. The clause, "we that are alive, that are left," is not a formal statement directly asserting that some of them would certainly be alive and be left, but is a statement adapted to any time in the indefinite future when the event referred to should occur and find Christians living. "We that are alive" is equivalent to the general expression, "all believers who are living at that time," which would include the speaker if he were then living. Secondly, in such phrases as "the Lord is at hand," we are bound to remember that man's estimate of periods of time must be relative. When projected upon the background of eternity, a thousand years become as a

---

[1] See chapter x.

day and a day as a thousand years.[1] Thirdly, the coming of the Lord is most likely a compound fact, including in the vision of the holy seer such all-important (to those who are specially concerned) providential events as the advent of death to the individual, the calamities connected with the destruction of Jerusalem (which closed the old dispensation), as well as the consummation of earthly history in the final judgment. But, fourthly, Paul himself should be allowed to interpret his own language, and in 2 Thess. ii. 2, 3 (written only a short time afterwards) he expressly intimates that either his readers had misunderstood his words or had been imposed upon by a forged letter: [2] "Be not quickly shaken from your mind, nor yet be troubled, either by spirit, or by word, or by Epistle as from us, as that the day of the Lord is *now present*; [3] let no man beguile you in any wise: for *it will not be*, except the falling away come first, and the man of sin be revealed, the son of perdition."

The passages in the New Testament seeming to teach that the second coming of Christ was to occur within a few years, should be interpreted so as to be consistent with everything else said in the Bible, and especially by the same writers upon the subject. We believe in the inspired word, not in every confident interpreter of that word. When

[1] 2 Peter iii. 8.

an interpreter affirms that Matthew xxiv. contains erroneous teaching concerning the time of the second coming of Christ, we are inclined to ask for the grounds of confidence upon which the interpreter bases his views. The interpreter is confident either that Christ was in error or that the evangelist misreported him. But in order to make this assertion he must be well assured of his own interpretation of the words. On the contrary, we distrust the confident dogmatism of those who affirm error here either in the teaching of Christ or in the report of the evangelists. The principles of interpretation revealed in the preceding paragraphs, and fully employed by Christ and the apostles, give ample warrant for that interpretation of the second coming of Christ which sees in it both type and antitype, and which recognizes the coming of Christ for judgment not only in the culminating crises of individual, social, and national life, but also in a final consummation of the history of the world,—these inferior crises being in their measure true specimens and representatives of the final catastrophe.

80. It may seem to some that, in presenting the subject occupying the preceding paragraphs first, we have reversed the natural order, having put that at the beginning of our remarks upon the interpretation of the Bible which is the consummate fruit of prolonged and tedious processes of

study. This is, however, the order in which we are all compelled to approach the subject. No man brought up in a Christian land can divest himself of prepossessions regarding Christianity. And while it is important for the student to prove all things, it is a matter of economy to pay great respect to the opinions already in possession of the field, and to secure correct knowledge in the first place, as to what those opinions are, and in the second place, as to the arguments by which they are supported. For purposes of investigation such a provisional acceptance of the results obtained by the work of former scholars, and practically verified by the abundant experience of the church, is of great advantage. The presumption is pretty strong that these results are in the main correct. Such confidence in the results of former investigation and experience gives steadiness also to our purposes while subjecting minor portions of the argument to the keen scrutiny of tentative criticism. We will therefore now take a rapid glance at some of the processes by which we approach the full meaning of the Bible and obtain at each step an authoritative view of its significance.

81. It is necessary at the outset for the interpreter to have an intelligent confidence in the text of Scripture which he endeavors to interpret. As already remarked, however, there is so nearly a general consent of specially qualified textual critics

to the genuineness of ninety-nine one-hundredths of the Bible that the textual uncertainty is reduced to very small limits, and, if we choose, we may set aside these uncertain points, and have undisputed possession of nearly the whole field. Perhaps there is also need of emphasizing the fact that, even without a knowledge of the original languages, the English reader has a sufficient variety of translations to form a safe judgment as to the main doctrines of Christianity. The dependence of the English reader upon translations is not altogether different from that of the ordinary Greek or Hebrew scholar upon the biblical critics and lexicographers. The student of the original languages of Scripture who is led by the knowledge given in this study to devote a large part of his time to solving the more intricate problems in textual criticism and interpretation, is in imminent danger of missing the main point, and of tithing mint, anise, and cummin, to the neglect of the weightier matters of the law.

Accepting intelligently the text before him the interpreter proceeds to ascertain the meaning of the individual words and sentences composing the volume. In this examination the investigator at once perceives that there is no cast-iron rigidity to language. The dictionary and the grammar do not weigh words for us, as the apothecary weighs medicine: nor is the stamp by which meaning is impressed upon words of the same character with that at the mint which leaves its impress upon coin. This fact concerning language is of twofold significance. In the first place, it makes a demand upon the patience of the interpreter in comparing with one another the various passages of the literature in which a word occurs, in order to ascertain for himself what peculiarities usage has impressed upon it. The etymology of a word and its original import count for little as compared with its use in contemporary literature. The lexicon gives us the opinion of the lexicographer as to the meaning of a word. That, however, is only an opinion formed by a more or less extensive examination of the passages in the literature where the word occurs. Every good lexicon contains abundant references to such passages and thus greatly facilitates our work. With the facilities thus afforded by the lexicons and grammars of the present day, it is a reasonably easy task to form by direct investigation a correct and independent judgment as to the meaning of all the more important words in biblical literature. So this apparent indefiniteness of language need not seriously interfere with the certainty of our opinions upon the main points of biblical teaching.

82. Due appreciation of the elasticity of words within moderate limits also enables us to correct a great number of the current assertions of inac-

curacy in the Bible. The failure to appreciate the reasonable elasticity of words is what gives rise to the larger part of the objections arising from alleged discrepancies. The so-called mistakes of the Bible can, for the most part, be shown to be in reality the mistakes of the interpreters.

For example, the apparent discrepancy concerning the healing of the blind men near Jericho [1] probably disappears when the elastic usage of a single word *engizein* (ἐγγίζειν)[2] is considered. This word bears the translation "to *be* near," as well as that of "to *come* near," and is frequently so used in the Septuagint. In 1 Kings xxi. 2, for example, Ahab is said to have desired Naboth's Vineyard because it was *near unto* his house (ἐγγίζειν). So that we are not compelled to understand Luke as saying that the miracle was performed as Christ was first entering into the city.[3] This, however, is but one mode of removing the apparent discrepancy, and is not without its difficulties,[4] the most serious of which is that Luke xix. 1 seems to say that afterwards Jesus entered into and went through Jericho. Any one, however, who attempts to write a brief, readable narrative will see how difficult it is to bring out everything in its

---

[1] Matt. xx. 29–34; Mark x. 46–52; Luke xviii. 35–43.
[2] Luke xviii. 35.
[3] See Robinson's Harmony.
[4] See Gardiner's Harmony, Andrews' Life of our Lord, and the commentators.

exact chronological order without both making the story dull and directing attention away from the main point by giving the chronological sequence more importance than rightfully belongs to it; hence, in rapid narrative, the necessity of frequently anticipating facts, and then referring to them in recapitulations. Let any one notice how often in narrating even simple events the thread of the story will carry him on beyond an important chronological point; and in order to pick up the story again he must inject a word or two of recapitulation — sometimes explicitly adding the phrase "to go back a little," sometimes not. Due regard to the necessity of vivid narrative will remove all occasion for asserting a discrepancy in the record under consideration.

83. By way of further illustration, we will consider perhaps the most serious discrepancy urged as existing between the statements of John and the other three evangelists. We refer to the question whether, on the evening before the crucifixion, Christ regularly ate the paschal supper with his disciples. The main facts are as follows: According to John xiii. 1 the Lord's Supper must have been instituted before the passover; according to John xviii. 28, the Jews were expecting to eat the passover when Christ was crucified; according to John xix. 14, the preparation of the passover was still in progress, and in verse 31

John calls it "a high day"; whereas, according to the other evangelists,[1] Jesus ate the passover with his disciples the evening before his arrest. Here seems to be a flat contradiction. But upon taking a closer view of the case, and examining more minutely into the meaning of the words, it appears that none of them have that cast-iron rigidity asserted by those who insist upon the contradiction. In the first place, we find from examining the literature of the subject that the word "passover" was used with somewhat of the same freedom as the word "thanksgiving" may be in New England, or the word "tea" in general society. Not long since the writer asked a friend if he would come to his house, at a certain time, and "take tea." The friend replied that he would, and it was reported in letters written the next day that he really did so. But when at the table this gentleman was asked if he would "take tea," he replied, "No, I thank you; please let me have some warm water." So another member of the family reported that this gentleman did *not take tea* at our house. If the letters containing these reports should be preserved for some future critic, they may give rise to an inconclusive discussion of the question, "Did the gentleman mentioned take tea or did he not take tea?" and such very likely is the question before us respecting the fact of

---

[1] Matt. xxvi. 17-30; Mark xiv. 12-26; Luke xxii. 1-20.

Christ's eating the passover with his disciples. At any rate, it would be very difficult for those who urge the contradiction to prove that the question is very much more difficult of solution than the one presented in the illustration just given might be. An examination of the usage of the word "passover" shows that in some places it means the passover lamb itself, and "to eat the passover" means to eat the paschal lamb.[1] In other places the word "passover" means the whole meal at which the paschal lamb was eaten,[2] as our word "tea" may refer to the whole meal at which tea is ordinarily served. Again, the word "passover" stands for the whole festival of the week in which the paschal lamb was slain.[3] Or again, "passover" may mean paschal sacrifices.[4] Again, the word "eat" in John xviii. 28 has an elasticity corresponding to "take" in the illustration just given. To "*eat* the passover" may very naturally have come to mean about the same as to "*keep* the passover"; so it seems to be used in 2 Chron. xxx. 18, 22. Due consideration of the usage of the words employed in this whole account makes it impossible to affirm a contradiction here between John and the other evangelists. We can easily

---

[1] Mark xiv. 12; Luke xxii. 7; 1 Cor. v. 7.
[2] Matt. xxvi. 18, 19; Luke xxii. 8, 13; Heb. xi. 28.
[3] Luke xxii. 1; Matt. xxvi. 2; John ii. 13; vi. 4.
[4] Compare Ps. cxviii. 27; Ex. xxiii. 18; Mal. ii. 3; 2 Chron. xxx. 22.

see that if we knew a little more than we do we might even be able to affirm an undesigned coincidence of great evidential value.

84. The liability to such indefiniteness in the use of language as we have just alluded to, is inevitable. But, as candid consideration will show, the only emergencies in which it need lead to serious doubts are where the literature of the subject is scanty, and where efforts are made to force a many-sided doctrine into a single formal statement. The safety with which the doctrines and facts of the Bible have been preserved to the world is largely owing to the extent and variety of the literature in which they are preserved and urged upon the attention of the world, and the extent of the disagreement among the interpreters of the Bible is often greatly magnified in popular statements.

Undue emphasis is laid in many quarters upon the imperfection of language as a means of conveying thought, and the danger of error in relying upon proof-texts for the support of doctrine has been unduly dwelt upon. It is true that occasionally doctrines have been supported by proof-texts which were entirely irrelevant. Still, the precise and definite words of the Bible are the best indexes we can have of the divine thoughts entering into the plan of salvation. Those who would erect alongside of the words of Scripture a co-ordinate authority variously called "Christian faith," "Christian consciousness," and "ethico-religious consciousness," are substituting shadows for substance, theories for facts, and ill-defined sentiments for the sure word of God.

When we are tempted to think lightly of the verbal revelation left us in the Bible, it would be well for us to pause and reflect upon the extent to which, in all the relations of life, we are dependent upon words for the conveyance of rights and privileges. In the language of another: "There is no title that is not conveyed by words. The houses we live in, the clothes we wear, the food we eat — these are obtained for us by words. By words are the great institutions of mercy and education about us shaped. Here is a deed, for instance, endowing a hospital on certain trusts, and through the words of these trusts the donor transmits curative and soothing power to multitudes of sick and wounded brought within those beneficent gates. And here is a will giving an educational fund to a college, and through the words of this will, stream encouragement and instruction to multitudes of poor scholars. Nor is this all. By words our great political safeguards are constructed. The words of the *habeas corpus* statute operate, wherever it is in force, to check arbitrary arrests. The words of the Bill of Rights attached to the Constitution of the United States, and of its several amendments, secure to each citizen of the United States protection in his civil relations; and through these words flow what we may venture to call grace from the people collectively as the source of power to the people individually as the enjoyers of rights. It is irrational, therefore, to denounce the Protestant view of the Bible as unduly assigning grace to words, when it is through the grace of words that we hold whatever rights we enjoy. Yet, on the other hand, it is equally irrational to talk of the words in the sacred text as though they transcended criticism, were insoluble by time, and operated mechanically and not dynamically. The divine revelation is just what we should suppose it would be, judging from the analogies of human law. Its words may sometimes be ambiguous. They are open to the modifications of time. There may be always a question as to what objects they apply. Yet through these words grace flows." [1]

85. The supposed modern improvements in the science of interpretation are to a considerable extent illusory. There have been no discoveries relating to that science at all to be compared with the discoveries in astronomy and geology. The scholars of the sixteenth century knew the Greek about as well as we do of the nineteenth. Calvin is still one of the best of commentators. But no

[1] Rev. Francis Wharton, LL.D., in *Bibliotheca Sacra*, Vol. xl. p. 217.

scientific man of his day, not even Copernicus, can be compared in his equipment with those of the present time. On the other hand, fifty-nine sixtieths of all the literature of the New Testament was in the hands of the reformers of Calvin's time, and the characteristics of modern interpretation have been exemplified by enlightened scholars in all ages of church history. The enlightened interpreter considers Scripture (according to the modern formula) *minutely, grammatically, contextually,* and *historically.* Nothing in a sentence, or a word even, is unworthy of careful attention from the interpreter. It will be remembered, for example, that when speaking of textual criticism instances were adduced in which the presence or absence of a single letter in a word produces marked results in the interpretation of a passage. Upon the presence or absence of the article before the word for feast (ἑορτή) in John v. 1, has been supposed to depend a whole year in the chronology of Christ's ministry. Careful attention to the grammar is of course essential, in order to obtain the natural meaning of the language; but, as already remarked, the meaning of the words themselves is largely dependent upon the context; so that a consideration of the context becomes a matter of prime necessity.

A word is as dependent upon the context for its shade of meaning as a house is upon its surroundings for the appropriate style of architecture. In determining the meaning of a word a variety of considerations come in play; the general style of the writer must be considered, as well as the known nature of the subject to which the language is applied. In poetry, where the necessities of metre and rhyme, or, as in Hebrew, of the parallelisms of thought, come into play, the construction of the language will be much less strict than in prose. We may expect the language of deep emotion to be figurative; while the same words in narrative speech would bear to be taken more nearly in their literal sense. In short, the known nature of the subject — however the knowledge is obtained — necessitates important modifications in our understanding of the words employed; that is, we assume that an intelligent writer would have his words interpreted with reference to all he is known to believe on the subject. If, for example, a man says, "Bring me the book," he means, bring it by some physical agency, because that is the only agency that can move a material object. If the judge says, "Bring the prisoner to the bar," his command involves the use of the motives that ordinarily control the movements of a prisoner. If a father says to his son, "Bring your friends to dinner," the use of physical force or of appeals to the fears of the friend, are excluded from our thoughts by the known relations of the parties. There is a long list of words in the New Testament which became so magnetized by their contact with Christianity that the classic Greek would find it difficult to recognize their meaning. The writers of the New Testament were compelled to do what they themselves said could not be done, namely, to put new wine into old wine-skins without bursting the skins. To a greater extent than any other book, the words of the New Testament receive their meaning from a great historical movement. The writers were called upon to clothe the peculiar and sublime religious thought of the Hebrews in the more decorous drapery of the Greek language. Yes, more than this; they were compelled to provide language for unheard-of and supernatural doctrines now for the first time revealed. Let any one compare classic Greek with the Greek of the New Testament, and he cannot fail to be impressed by the enlargement in every dimension of thought which has taken place in such words as πίστις (faith), δικαιόω (to make righteous or to justify), ἅγιος (holy), καλεῖν (to call, from which comes the word "elect"), ἀγάπη (love), ἐλπίς (hope), χάρις (grace), εὐαγγέλιον (gospel), ψυχή (life), κηρύσσειν (to preach), ἀπόστολος (apostle), πρεσβύτερος (elder), ἐπίσκοπος (bishop), διάκονος (deacon), βαπτίζειν (to baptize), κοινωνία (fellowship), σάρξ (flesh), σωτηρία (salvation), λυτροῦσθαι (to redeem), καταλλάσσειν (to reconcile), παλιγγενεσία (regeneration), φῶς (light).

All these words, and many others, have been unspeakably enriched and permanently enlarged in their meaning by their adoption into Christianity. The process by which such words are transformed is familiar enough; though it has never been illustrated elsewhere upon so grand a scale. Unlike silver and gold, words are wholly dependent for their value upon the stamp which is on them, that is, usage determines the meaning of a word. Words have value and power in proportion to the nobility of the things to which they are habitually applied and to the importance of the connection in which they are habitually used. In far too many cases words which have come to have an exalted meaning gradually lose it, because the people using them are no longer performing noble deeds or cherishing noble objects of contemplation. It is thus that charity (as depicted in 1 Cor. xiii.), which in our own language signified the sum of all Christian virtue, has degenerated to signify that single form of benevolence in which we give money to relieve the wants of men. But, on the other hand, there are periods of history characterized by so many noble deeds that old words take on new meanings, and the whole language of a people becomes instinct with new life. It is in such periods of history that we witness the most remarkable outbursts of literary activity. But no other quickening of national life is to be compared in its effect on language, with that baptism of the Greek tongue which it received on the occasion of its contact with the ineffable realities connected with the incarnation of Christ and the outpouring of the Holy Spirit under the Christian dispensation.

86. It is not, however, by any means always easy to define accurately the meaning of single terms and phrases; for when taken out of their connection the words often lose that lustre of reflected light which belongs to them in connected discourse. The shade of meaning belonging to a word can be determined only by considering the whole context. There are no absolute rules by which to demonstrate the meaning of a sentence, as one would the truth of an algebraic formula. To carry conviction as to the truth of any particular interpretation we must depend upon the facts themselves, somewhat as we would convince another of the beauty of a statue by disclosing to his view the object itself. But even in this case something more is necessary than the mere removing of a veil. To secure unanimity of judgment it is essential that the beholders have the same normal powers of vision, and have patience to look at the object with the same degree of attention and the will to observe it from the same points of view. If one persists in examining a statue with a micro-

scope and sounding it with a geological hammer, we need not be surprised if he fails to discover the beauty which another discerns who examines it from an artistic point of view.

No one would care to disguise the fact that the Bible may be misapprehended; that it may be examined in such a way that its majestic power shall be undiscovered and its matchless beauty undiscerned. The Bible is literature, and is instinct with living thought. The thought of a book, like the life of a plant or animal, cannot be obtained by dissection or chemical analysis. In these mechanical processes we destroy the subtile power of life that made it an organic whole.

In dwelling thus, however, upon the danger of subjecting the words of Scripture to the mechanical processes of mere literal interpretation, we do not discredit the power of language to convey definite thought, and to preserve it in fixed forms as an heirloom to successive ages; for such power it most certainly has, the Bible itself being, in fact, one of the most striking illustrations of the power of language to move the world. The difficulty encountered in this case is to hold the attention of individual students to the facts of the Bible considered together and as a whole.

As before remarked we are in great danger of overestimating the extent of disagreement between interpreters, and of underestimating the number and importance of the points in which Christian believers are agreed. The history of the evangelical portion of the church has revolved in a pretty narrow orbit about three cardinal doctrines of the Bible. The tendencies to aberration have, for the great mass of believers, been from time to time counteracted, so that the heart of evangelical Christendom has remained true, and her faith in these three doctrines remained constant. During every age, however, there have been local companies of individuals who have strayed so far from the attracting power that they have gone off at a tangent, and, like the comets, become wandering orbs whose movements defy calculation.

The three doctrines to which we refer are 1st. That God has made a special historical revelation to men, and that the Bible is the authoritative record of that revelation. 2d. That the incarnation and death of Christ are sacrificial in their character, and were necessary, as well in justification of God's action in forgiving sin as in furnishing a moral power for securing the obedience of the individual sinner. 3d. That this world is the arena on which human beings determine the conditions of their existence for an endless futurity. Apart from these doctrines there has been little evangelical activity in the world.

87. An important question upon which Protestants and Catholics differ relates to the intelligibility

of the Bible, both agreeing that the real teaching of the Bible upon moral and religious questions is without error. But the Catholic maintains that a special body of divinely aided interpreters (of which the pope is now the representative) is essential to the discovery and exposition of the Scriptures; whereas, Protestants insist on placing the Bible in the hands of the common people, — having confidence that the general good sense of those who read, as it is aided by the free discussion of scholars, the divinely ordered progress of events, and the pervasive witness of the Holy Spirit, will obtain a sufficient understanding of it to secure not only individual salvation, but their growth in grace and their preparation for attaining all the high purposes of their spiritual calling. That portions of the Scriptures have been grossly misunderstood, and perverted to ignoble and unworthy uses, is no more proof of inherent fallibility than are the perversions to which the laws of nature are subject. It is a part of our moral trial in this world to wait patiently while exercising all our powers to ascertain what is the will of God as expressed both in nature and the Bible. If a stone has proved to us a stone of stumbling, it is to teach us to step higher and walk more carefully. If a portion of Scripture has conveyed to us a false impression, and been perverted to sustain us in our adherence to false doctrine, it is to teach us a lesson in humility. We are not to suppose that the few things of which we are assured in the present low stage of our development exhaust the teachings of the Bible, or that the unexplored remnants of Scripture have yielded all their treasure.

But what, as Protestants, we do hold is that the Bible is the word of God, and is the revelation in human language to which we must go for the doctrines which are the basis of all our Christian activity; and that by its teachings we are to test all our religious theories and hold in check all our moral speculations. To those who put forward with special authority their ethico-religious consciousness, we say, in the language of the prophet when speaking of the utterances of those who in his time professed communion with spirits, "To the law and to the testimony: if they speak not according to this word *it is* because there is no light in them."[1] In submitting to the guidance of the Bible we are doing what the scientific man does, who subordinates his theories to the facts of nature. Those facts may be difficult of interpretation but they are realities, and yield the truth so far as he understands them; while their hidden meaning is ever beckoning him on to further investigation into the real nature of things. The difference between the interpreter who acknowledges the Bible as supreme authority and the one

[1] Isa. viii. 20.

who exalts his own ethico-religious consciousness to that place of authority is about the same as that between the sea-captain who takes his bearings from the stars and the one who guides his course by the light upon his own masthead.

VIII.

SUMMARY OF THE POSITIVE ARGUMENT.

88. So far it has been our object to bring into one view the positive arguments which convince a believer in the Bible of its inspiration and divine authority. The arguments for its divine authority are drawn chiefly from the Bible itself, and will have little weight with those who do not accept the general credibility of the book. To the believer in the authenticity of the Bible, however, the considerations presented ought to be conclusive; for the authenticity of the Bible is bound up with its inspiration.

We would not, however, be understood as affirming that there are no difficulties in the way of those who receive the Bible as of divine authority throughout. We do not accept the inspiration of the Bible under the delusion, that everything pertaining to the subject can be made perfectly clear; but rather we feel warranted in accepting the ordinary doctrine of inspiration as here set forth, because the difficulties connected with that theory are so small and so few in comparison with those encountered upon any other theory. It is easier to reject the supernatural claims of Christianity entirely than to accept those claims, and call ourselves Christians, while attempting to explain away as of little meaning the remarkable language of the sacred writers concerning themselves. The part of a reasonable man in such a situation is, to move onward with confidence in the line of least resistance, and, if difficulties meet him, to fortify his assurance by reflecting how much greater difficulties would be encountered in any other direction.

89. Briefly stated, the evangelical theory of the inspiration of the Bible rests upon the fourfold fact: *a*. That Christianity is essentially supernatural, involving the incarnation of the Second Person of the divine Trinity, and his miraculous entrance into, and miraculous exit from, the world. This removes antecedent objections. *b*. It is appropriate and important, not to say necessary, that the record of such a divine intervention in history should be adequate, and free from essential error, lest the intervention itself should fail to accomplish its end. This makes the fact of inspiration antecedently probable. *c*. Such emphatic promises of assistance were given by Christ to the apostles and their associates, upon whom would come the responsibility of recording the facts and unfolding the doctrines essential to Christianity,

SUMMARY OF THE POSITIVE ARGUMENT. 153

that we look to find these promises fulfilled in the writings of the apostles. *d.* The repeated assertion by certain of the writers of the New Testament, that they wrote by divine authority, coupled with the fact that in all their writings and conduct they both assume and assert that the Old Testament is the inspired word of God, compels us to accept large portions of the New Testament as inspired or reject it altogether. The opinion of the Old Testament entertained by the writers of the New, becomes the standard by which we are to measure the estimate set upon the books of the New Testament by the primitive church. We cannot suppose that the churches of the first and second centuries could accord a lower place to the books which they accepted as containing the authoritative accounts of Christian fact and doctrine, written by the apostles and their associates under the conditions we have described, than was accorded to the Old Testament Scriptures.

90. Some may think that too great weight is given to the testimony of the churches of the first and second centuries concerning the authority of the books of the New Testament. A little reflection, however, will show that the churches of the first and second centuries were the proper judges and the natural guardians of the earliest Christian records, and that the testimony which they have borne to the records we have is not easily contra-

dicted or disturbed. During the first two centuries of the Christian era, the traditional knowledge of the facts and doctrines of Christianity must have been remarkably fresh; so that the churches could then judge, as no one at a later day would be able to do, whether the purported documents claiming authoritative recognition agreed with the testimony and preaching with which the original churches were familiar. The teachers of Justin Martyr, of Irenæus, and of Clement of Alexandria, were the contemporaries of some of the apostles; and the majority of the books of the New Testament are witnessed to by these three great writers and their contemporaries of the second century, as worthy of unquestioned confidence and as being actually received as such by the churches of their time. The believers of that period appeal to those books and quote them with the same deference with which both Jews and Christians treated the Old Testament.

91. It is no slight confirmatory evidence of the authority of the books of the New Testament as we now have it, that in intrinsic character they stand so far above all other literature of their time. They really have no competitors. The apocryphal Gospels are silly and puerile in the extreme, teaching no important moral lessons, revealing no important truth, and abounding in miracles utterly foreign to the spirit and dignity of the Gospels.

SUMMARY OF THE POSITIVE ARGUMENT. 155

The Epistles of Clement and Barnabas bear no comparison, in point of intrinsic excellence, with the Epistles of Paul, Peter, James, and John.

92. The doubts and hesitancy through which several of the books of the New Testament obtained general recognition from the churches, increase rather than diminish our confidence in the final decision; for it shows that the early Christians were not inclined to act in so weighty a matter, except upon the best of evidence. Before the close of the fourth century of the present era entire unanimity was attained by the churches in recognizing the authority of all the present books of the New Testament. Before the beginning of the third century, or within one hundred years of the death of the apostle John, there was entire agreement throughout the churches in accepting as authoritative the larger part of the New Testament; while the hesitancy manifested in some quarters about accepting a part of the remainder is matched by abundant positive testimony to the acceptance in other quarters.

93. We do not dispute the right of any one to attempt to reverse the judgment of the primitive church concerning books admitted into the New Testament; but we insist, that such a one shall recognize the difficulty of his undertaking. To come into court after sixteen hundred years have elapsed, and attempt to reverse the decision ren-

dered by the jury when the facts were fresh, when evidence was accessible, and when the truth was accepted at the hazard of one's life, requires no small degree of self-assurance. Such reversal of judgment can be secured only on the discovery of very cogent evidence. To us the difficulties of explaining away the evidence ascribing to the Old and New Testaments in their sphere infallible authority, seem insuperable. The argument endures every scientific test that can be applied to the subject, and the case seems proved, unless we discard the whole idea of a supernatural intervention, and consider Christianity as resting throughout upon a delusion.

We will turn now to consider more at length some of the difficulties which lie in the way of accepting the doctrine that the Scriptures are, throughout, the product of divine inspiration, and to answer in detail some of the objections which with more or less force are urged against the doctrine.

IX.

INHERENT DIFFICULTIES OF THE SUBJECT.

94. Many of the objections urged against the doctrine of inspiration are inherent in the nature of the subject, and arise from attempting to define the *mode* of inspiration more minutely than we are authorized to do. In this, as in other matters, we have, as before remarked, far more practical interest in the end secured than in the process through which it is attained, and we should be cautious about attempting to limit God in the manner of his operations. The revelation of the Infinite Being to his creatures and his manifestation in time and space, involve essential mysteries which the human mind may not hope to fathom.

95. The doctrine that the Bible is the word of God throughout, and that in all its parts it is the product of that special divine forethought and activity comprehensively styled "inspiration," involves almost exactly the same difficulties with the doctrine that nature is the product of design, and is throughout a revelation of divine wisdom. In recent times we have enlarged beyond measure our

knowledge of the mode by which God works to accomplish his designs in nature; and there has been a pretty widespread apprehension that, upon the discovery of the *processes* or the *laws* of nature, we shall lose the idea of the *design* in nature. The futility of such fears we have elsewhere shown.[1] As a brilliant essayist has remarked,[2] "It is a singular fact, that whenever we find out how anything is done our conclusion seems to be that God did not do it."

96. It is an unpardonable error, however, to assume that God's designs cannot be accomplished by more recondite and indirect methods than those which would be pursued by men. God makes a horse by a much more roundabout and complicated process than is pursued by a mechanic in making a clock. The discovery of the vast distances of the stars from us, and that the phenomena of the seasons and of day and night are produced by movements of the earth rather than by the revolution of the heavens, and that the courses of the heavenly orbs are determined by the law of gravitation, and that God's designs are far more comprehensive than was formerly supposed, should enlarge our conception of God's power and wisdom rather than diminish our sense of his nearness to us.

---

[1] See the author's Logic of Christian Evidences, pp. 73-122, and Studies in Science and Religion, pp. 165-255.
[2] Frances Power Cobbe.

97. A line of remark similar to the foregoing is eminently appropriate respecting the doctrine of the inspiration of Scripture. We should not embarrass ourselves with any theory of inspiration based largely upon the etymology of the word. When we speak of Scripture as "inspired," or "God-breathed," we are using language after the manner of men, and the word should receive that modification of meaning which all words have when made to describe the being or the actions of God. The evidence of inspiration adduced in the preceding chapters bears upon the end secured rather than upon the divine method of attaining the end. In old times God spoke unto the fathers through the prophets, "by divers portions and in divers manners."[1] We are not seriously concerned with the question whether a portion of Scripture is made authoritative by the direct suggestion of the Spirit to the writer, or by a superintendence which keeps the writer from incorporating what is essentially erroneous and misleading. The important question is, Is the Bible perfect as related to the end it has in view? viz. to provide the world with a permanently adequate, authoritative, and intelligible historical record of the supernatural revelation of himself made in connection with the incarnation of Christ? In thus viewing the question we shall find little difficulty in understanding

[1] Heb. i. 1.

the subject, so far as our duty and welfare are concerned.

98. Doubtless God has an indefinite variety of ways by which to secure the perfection which characterizes the Scriptures of the Old and New Testaments. A part of the perfection of these writings for their designed purpose must have been secured by direct suggestion, illumination, and revelation; while upon their human side, as adapted to finite apprehension, much of the perfection of Scripture consists in the purely natural and human elements which have been incorporated and adopted as a part of the instrument of divine revelation. In this respect the Bible may be compared to the person of Christ, which combines in mysterious union both human and divine elements. It has always been a matter of difficulty, in forming a conception of Christ's nature, to keep one of these elements from overshadowing or absorbing the other. In contemplating the divine element of Christ's nature the humanity is in danger of fading from our vision. It was, for example, the doctrine of the Doketæ — an heretical sect which flourished toward the close of the second century — that "Christ had no real body; his appearance in the actual world was only a magical apparition, his body a phantom, his birth and death, visions."[1] Representatives of this heretical genus, which so

---

[1] Schaff-Herzog Encyclopædia, article Doketism.

exalts the divine as to abolish the human, and so conceives of the infinite as to render the finite impossible, appear in the history of the doctrine of inspiration. Certain theologians in the latter part of the seventeenth, and the beginning of the eighteenth, century — of whom the Buxtorfs, the Carpzovs, and Quenstedt, are representatives — compared the sacred writers to pens or flutes, thus rendering their personality absolutely quiescent, and making the human element in the Scriptures a direct product of divine action.

99. On the other hand, as we are inclined to reject the divinity of Christ when contemplating his humanity, so we are in danger of eliminating the conception of a pervasive divine element from Scripture. As Christ would not have been God *manifest in the flesh* except his humanity had been perfect, so the Bible would not be the *word of God* except there were a purely human element in it, to which the divine word has become indissolubly joined. Our theory of inspiration, therefore, simply involves the perfection of the Bible for its designed purpose, which is, as already remarked, to give to the world a permanent, adequate, intelligible, and authoritative written revelation of religious truth. As such we receive it on the strength of the positive evidence already presented.

We will now attend to the objections urged against this view of the Bible; and the reader is asked to consider whether the difficulties in the way of accepting the Bible as the inspired word of God are not far less than those involved in the rejection of its inspiration, compelling us to explain away all the evidence heretofore presented.

100. Before considering more in detail the reality of the discrepancies of various sorts so freely alleged to exist in the Bible, it is well to remind ourselves again that a considerable amount of seeming error in the Bible is eliminated by scientific criticism of the text, and so is shown to belong to the transcribers, and not to the original writers. A still larger portion of seeming errors is the result of unscientific habits of interpretation. But after the true text is approximately determined, and the true interpretation secured with a reasonable degree of certainty, there may still be in the literature conveying the precious spiritual thought a residuum of erroneous conceptions relating to minor and irrelative points, which would not affect at all the absolute truth of the teaching upon the main points. The presence of such errors is accounted for on the principle of accommodation, and in reality is far from being a literary imperfection. The true theory of accommodation admits of the incorporation of many apparently false conceptions into the literary forms by which divine truth is expressed. This approval of false conceptions will, however, be a matter of appear-

ance rather than of reality. Since man is finite and at the outset perfectly ignorant, his increase in knowledge is necessarily gradual, and so it is not possible to teach him everything at once. The wise teacher, therefore, concentrates the attention of his pupils upon one thing at a time, and does not meanwhile disturb the preconceived notions entertained upon subsidiary and minor points; but by thus leaving minor errors unchallenged the teacher is far from endorsing them.

Indeed, in popular literature an inordinate amount of attention to secure minutely exact statements of the subsidiary facts casually alluded to in the main discourse, is itself one of the most serious of rhetorical errors, and inevitably leads to a misapprehension of the importance of the principal points to be impressed; hence, for example, in Scripture and everywhere the abundant use of round numbers. When a writer refers to something as having occurred fifty years ago, it depends upon the character of the literature whether we are to understand him as stating an exact number of years or only as referring to a long but rather indefinite period. It is the province of the interpreter to determine from close examination of the literature in which they occur, how exact the individual statements are meant to be. Words should not be pressed in poetry as in prose, and in a popular address we should not expect the same attempt at accuracy that would be necessary in a scientific treatise. An oil painting should not be scrutinized too closely. It is made for general effect at an appropriate distance, and not for microscopical examination.

101. Every person in ordinary conversation apparently gives countenance to innumerable errors. In most cases, however, it is readily seen that such errors belong to the costume of speech, and are not really adopted by us. When we speak of a "lunatic asylum" no one would now think of imputing to us the notion that mental derangement is produced by the influence of the moon, though that is the theory underlying the etymology of the word, and the word came into its present use because the erroneous theory was once generally believed. Within the present generation the word "medium" has come into general use, and is employed without protest by those who do not wish in any manner to countenance the theory which has given rise to the word. The Spiritualists really hold that certain of their number become *mediums* of communication between the living and the dead. But the majority of people use the word without protestation and without the slightest intention of encouraging the error. It would be a useless affectation, and a waste of both time and space, to accompany the word "medium," everytime we had occasion to use it, with the

prefix "so-called." When an ordinary writer says "medium" every one knows that he means a *so-called* medium.

102. It is thus, no doubt, that Paul speaks[1] of the damsel at Philippi as having "a spirit of divination," literally of *Python*. It would certainly be unwarranted to attribute to Paul the full literal, or we would rather say the full etymological, meaning of this phrase; for then we should make him endorse the polytheism of the Greeks. His opinions are so pronounced and well known upon that subject, however, that there is no more danger of misunderstanding than when we use the word "lunatic" or "medium," or, without thinking of the medical theory involved, we speak of "catching cold." It is thus that Christ can say the mustard-seed is "less than all seeds"[2] without any danger of our mistaking it for an exact scientific statement. Likewise, when Moses speaks[3] of the coney as chewing the cud, and not parting the hoof, no one is troubled at finding that, though the exact truth is stated as to the hoof, and the coney is therefore an unclean animal, he does not in fact chew the cud, but only seems to do so — the coney being actually a rodent, and, like all that class, moving his jaws *as if chewing*

---

[1] Acts xvi. 16 sq.
[2] Matt. xiii. 31, 32; cf. Mark iv. 31.
[3] Lev. xi. 5.

the cud, but really for the purpose of wearing off his teeth and keeping them from becoming uncomfortably long. This movement of the jaws was popularly misunderstood, but was, nevertheless, one of the best signs by which to distinguish the animal, — which was all that was necessary for the purposes of the Mosaic reference.

It is not always easy to tell the precise limits of the sphere of this principle of accommodation in language; but the difficulty is no greater than universally exists in determining the boundary line between the figurative and the literal use of language. In general, however, there is little occasion for misunderstanding. It is as when night shades into day, or winter into spring, or the climate of the temperate zone into that of the torrid; there is a confusing border-line between the two, but it is narrow, and does by no means obscure the broad contrasts between the great classes of facts which are brought into comparison.

103. A manifestly extreme and erroneous attempt to apply the theory of accommodation is found in the efforts to explain the alleged demoniacal possessions (of which so much is said in the New Testament) as ordinary physical and mental affections, now treated in insane asylums. It is true that most of the phenomena of those who are said to have been possessed by demons can be matched in

INHERENT DIFFICULTIES OF THE SUBJECT. 167

modern records of insanity. But the same effects may be produced by a variety of causes. Apoplexy may be induced by excessive joy or grief. If the digestive organs are obstructed, the symptoms may be similar, whatever may be the primary cause of the obstruction. The specific cause producing disturbances in physiological or mental phenomena is not the only thing which determines the character of the effects. The principal factor in the production of such effects is to be found in the nature of the element disturbed. The obstruction causing a ripple in the stream may be a block of stone, or a mass of iron, or a water-soaked log of wood. So it is too much for us to affirm that physicians have even yet penetrated to the real cause of all mental diseases. The physical disturbances connected with mental disease, are only phenomena, for which we must ascribe a cause, and that cause may well enough be, in some cases, demoniacal possession.

Now, our belief in the reality of demoniacal possession in the time of Christ rests upon a variety of facts, involving the veracity of the entire New Testament. *a.* The writers distinguished demoniacs from those who were sick.[1] *b.* The demons are represented as speaking with supernatural knowledge of their own.[2] *c.* The demons

---

[1] Mark i. 32; Luke vi. 17, 18; Matt. iv. 24.
[2] Matt. viii. 29; Mark i. 24, 25; v. 7; Luke iv. 41.

at Gadara asked permission to go into a herd of swine.[1] The permission was granted. They went, and the results are well known. *d.* Christ repeatedly reasons[2] with his disciples on the supposition that demons are in the service of Satan, and adduces the power to cast them out (which he both exercises and bestows) as a sign that the kingdom of heaven had come. *e.* Most significant of all, Jesus *in private conversation* with the disciples repeatedly speaks as if the popular ideas on the subject were correct.[3]

The number and variety of these concessions to the prevailing view concerning demoniacal possession render it exceedingly difficult, not to say impossible, to explain them all away upon the theory of accommodation. It is not once or twice, but well-nigh a hundred times, that the matter is referred to. The popular error, if real, seems too serious to have been thus encouraged by him whose mission it was to bear witness to the truth; especially, as the connection shows, to that truth which was related to the way of salvation and life. Any one can see that the encouragement of superstition is a very different matter from merely allowing erroneous scientific conceptions to remain undisturbed, and it sustains a much more vital

---

[1] Matt. viii. 31; Mark v. 12; Luke viii. 32.
[2] Matt. xii. 24–32; Mark iii. 22–30; Luke x. 17–20; xi. 15–23.
[3] Matt. x. 8; xii. 43 sq.; Mark ix. 28, 29; Luke x. 18 sq.

relation to the great spiritual truths upon which our salvation depends. Thus, as we approach the central subjects of revelation, the divine veracity becomes more and more involved in the forms of statement.

104. It would be difficult to maintain respect for the New Testament writers if they were so uncritical that no dependence can be placed upon their explicit statements of facts. Before endeavoring, however, to state exactly the latitude of historical inaccuracy which might be compatible with the divine authority of their teachings upon moral and religious subjects, it is proper to ask how much of the alleged historical inaccuracy of the sacred writers is real, and how much is a figment of the critical imagination. There is scarcely any limit to the boldness of infidels and rash critics in asserting the existence of irreconcilable discrepancies in the Bible, and of attributing to it positive error of various kinds. Now, as in the days of the beloved disciple, we are in need of his wholesome advice: "Beloved, believe not every spirit, but prove the spirits, whether they are of God; because many false prophets are gone out into the world."[1]

The belief in the existence of an unlimited amount of discrepancy and error in the Bible is more likely to prevail because of the positiveness

[1] 1 John iv. 1.

Christ as "standing over her" when he rebuked the fever (without any intimation that he touched her); Matthew mentions that he "touched her hand," and the fever left her; while Mark adds that he " took her by the hand, and raised her up," and the fever left her. In this simple case it is easy enough to see how the testimony of the one supplements that of the other, and how each item of information can be worked into a consistent whole, and made to contribute to the vividness of the picture. Putting all the accounts together, it would read, "And he stood over her, and rebuked the fever, and touched her hand, and lifted her up, and immediately the fever left her, and she ministered unto them."

107. Nor is it only in describing scenes and actions that different words may be employed by different writers to convey a common fact. In reporting the remarks of another so as to convey their full meaning to a reader or to a different audience from that to which they were addressed, considerable liberty is allowable. For example, in the account of the stilling of the tempest, in the midst of which Christ had fallen asleep in the bottom of the ship,[1] Matthew represents the disciples as awakening him with the cry, "Save, Lord, we perish"; in Mark it reads, "Master, carest thou not that we perish?" while in Luke it is,

[1] Matt. viii. 25; Mark iv. 38; Luke viii. 24.

"Master, master, we perish." Now, in maintaining that we have here a correct account of what occurred, it is not necessary for us to suppose that these three exact forms of words were used upon that occasion. Indeed, it is probable that the words were not spoken in Greek, but in Aramaic, and so as we have them are only translations from the original. But even if they had been spoken in Greek, we only have to suppose (what is evident enough from their brevity) that each one is but a partial quotation of what numerous voices uttered, and of words to which the tones of voice and the attitudes of the speakers imparted a meaning which cannot be all transferred to the printed page by literal quotation. Again, in the Saviour's reply to them, the phrase in Matthew is, " Why are ye fearful, *O ye of little faith?*" in Mark, " Why are ye fearful? *have ye not yet faith?*" or according to the reading of some manuscripts, " *How is it that ye have no faith?*" Here, also, it is evident it cannot be affirmed that any one form of printed words exhausts the meaning of Christ's utterance. *O ye of little faith* may be said with a tone and inflection to convey all the meaning expressed in the phrase, *Have ye not yet faith?* Or, again, we can say — and that with a pretty high degree of certainty — that the reported laconic phrases of our Lord were probably not by any means all that he said upon that occasion. It is presumable that

Christ as "standing over her" when he rebuked the fever (without any intimation that he touched her); Matthew mentions that he "touched her hand," and the fever left her; while Mark adds that he "took her by the hand, and raised her up," and the fever left her. In this simple case it is easy enough to see how the testimony of the one supplements that of the other, and how each item of information can be worked into a consistent whole, and made to contribute to the vividness of the picture. Putting all the accounts together, it would read, "And he stood over her, and rebuked the fever, and touched her hand, and lifted her up, and immediately the fever left her, and she ministered unto them."

107. Nor is it only in describing scenes and actions that different words may be employed by different writers to convey a common fact. In reporting the remarks of another so as to convey their full meaning to a reader or to a different audience from that to which they were addressed, considerable liberty is allowable. For example, in the account of the stilling of the tempest, in the midst of which Christ had fallen asleep in the bottom of the ship,[1] Matthew represents the disciples as awakening him with the cry, "Save, Lord, we perish"; in Mark it reads, "Master, carest thou not that we perish?" while in Luke it is,

[1] Matt. viii. 25; Mark iv. 38; Luke viii. 24.

"Master, master, we perish." Now, in maintaining that we have here a correct account of what occurred, it is not necessary for us to suppose that these three exact forms of words were used upon that occasion. Indeed, it is probable that the words were not spoken in Greek, but in Aramaic, and so as we have them are only translations from the original. But even if they had been spoken in Greek, we only have to suppose (what is evident enough from their brevity) that each one is but a partial quotation of what numerous voices uttered, and of words to which the tones of voice and the attitudes of the speakers imparted a meaning which cannot be all transferred to the printed page by literal quotation. Again, in the Saviour's reply to them, the phrase in Matthew is, "Why are ye fearful, *O ye of little faith?*" in Mark, "Why are ye fearful? *have ye not yet faith?*" or according to the reading of some manuscripts, "*How is it that ye have no faith?*" Here, also, it is evident it cannot be affirmed that any one form of printed words exhausts the meaning of Christ's utterance. *O ye of little faith* may be said with a tone and inflection to convey all the meaning expressed in the phrase, *Have ye not yet faith?* Or, again, we can say — and that with a pretty high degree of certainty — that the reported laconic phrases of our Lord were probably not by any means all that he said upon that occasion. It is presumable that

Jesus uttered many words, as John assures us that he performed many miracles, "which are not written in this book," and that only such things are recorded as are necessary to lead us to a full faith that Jesus is the Christ, and that we may have life in his name.[1] In affirming or denying the perfection of the sacred record we are bound to remember the relative character of all perfection. In affirming perfection of any thing the object for which the thing exists must be kept in view. A perfect carriage wheel, for example, is far from being perfect when considered apart from its relation to the rest of the vehicle. The human eye is not perfect in itself, but only in its adaptations to the diversified composition of man — not only as he exists individually, but as he is propagated under a complicated physical law of inheritance. Nor in speaking of the perfection of God's work in the natural creation do we imply that equal perfection could not have been secured in another plan. So, also, the particular words chosen to express the designed ideas in revelation might, for aught we know, have been replaced by others equally good, but not by any which are better adapted to their purpose.

108. We are compelled to give more attention to the subject of alleged verbal discrepancies in Scripture than would otherwise be necessary, be-

[1] John xx. 30, 31.

cause of the mistaken prominence given to this class of objections by some recent writers,[1] who treat the question with little regard to the true logical principles involved. A few instances may, therefore, be treated here in greater detail than was proper when illustrating the processes of interpretation. It is, however, foreign to the design of the present discussion to consider at length every alleged discrepancy of the Bible. For such treatment the reader is referred to standard works on the subject.[2]

A prominent example introduced by Dr. Ladd among the irreconcilable discrepancies of the Gospels relates to the conversation of Christ with the rich young man.[3] In this narrative, according to the text which is now received, Matthew makes Christ say in reply to the young man, " Why asketh thou me concerning that which is good? One there is who is good"; while in Mark and Luke Christ's reply reads, " Why callest thou me good? None is good, save one, *even* God." Professor Ladd asserts that " both forms of the reply cannot be correct; and that in which Mark and Luke agree is doubtless the original one."[4] On the contrary, we may safely affirm that

[1] See especially The Doctrine of Sacred Scripture, by George T. Ladd, D.D.
[2] See especially Haley's Alleged Discrepancies of the Bible.
[3] Matt. xix. 17; Mark x. 18; Luke xviii. 19.
[4] Doctrine of Sacred Scripture, Vol. I. p. 401.

there is scarcely any difficulty at all in believing that both forms are correct. In order to warrant Professor Ladd's assertion, he must assume, without evidence and against all probability, that the evangelists pretended to give a complete account of all the conversation that took place between Christ and the rich young man; whereas, any one at all familiar with the dialectical processes naturally pursued in such a private conversation as this between Christ and the rich young man, can easily see that in an interview of half an hour, or ten minutes even, there was superabundant opportunity for all the expressions recorded in Matthew and Mark, and many more, to have been made.

109. Dr. Ladd likewise finds[1] a discrepancy between Matt. xix. 7 and Mark x. 3, because in one part of the discussion between Christ and the Pharisees respecting divorce, Christ himself appeals to Moses, and asks the Pharisees, "What did Moses command you?" and in another part of the conversation the Pharisees say unto him, "Why, then, did Moses command to give a bill of divorcement?" It is possible to find a discrepancy here only on the assumption that all the conversation upon that occasion consists of the one hundred and one words comprised in Matthew's report, with the addition of the few variations of Mark. This would reduce the interview to a period of about

[1] Doctrine of Sacred Scripture, Vol. I. p. 401.

two minutes; whereas, if they were ten minutes together — or five minutes even — there was ample room for all these variations which are thought to give so much trouble. We submit that it is altogether probable that the interview continued for a considerable time, and that the dialogue between Christ and the Pharisees, like a meandering stream, was continually shifting positions of attack and defence.

110. The same writer is also doubtful whether the four forms of the inscription over the cross can be verbally reconciled.[1] The facts concerning this are simply these: According to John,[2] the inscription on the cross was written in Hebrew, Latin, and Greek, — that is, there were three inscriptions, and that is just what seems to be given by the different evangelists. John records the inscription as "Jesus of Nazareth, the king of the Jews" (perhaps the Hebrew form); Matthew gives it as "This is Jesus, the king of the Jews" (perhaps the Greek form);[3] Mark gives it as simply "The king of the Jews" (perhaps, or we may say probably, the translation of the Latin inscription);[4] Luke agrees word for word with Mark, except that he adds the demonstrative pronoun "this" (οὗτος), which makes it read, "This is the king of the Jews,"[5] — a freedom which is perfectly allow-

---

[1] Doctrine of Sacred Scripture, Vol. I. p. 400.
[2] John xix. 20. [3] Matt. xxvii. 37.
[4] Mark xv. 26. [5] Luke xxiii. 38.

able in translating the two words, *Rex Judaeorum*, which would suffice in the terse Latin tongue.[1]

111. Perhaps the most difficult of all the apparent discrepancies in quoting the Saviour's language, occurs in the instructions given to the twelve when first sent out on their apostolic mission. We give the accounts in parallel columns:

MATT. X.	MARK VI.	LUKE IX.
9 Get you no gold, nor silver, nor brass 10 in your purses; no wallet for *your* journey, neither two coats, nor shoes, nor staff: for the laborer is worthy of his food.	8 And he charged them that they should take nothing for *their* journey, save a staff only: no bread, no wallet, no money in their purse; 9 but *to go* shod with sandals: and, *said he*, put not on two coats.	3 And he said unto them, Take nothing for your journey, neither staff, nor wallet, nor bread, nor money; neither have two coats.

Here we have a report of certain words spoken by Jesus to his disciples, upon one of the most important and solemn occasions of their lives. All told, Matthew gives to his entire summary of the discourse only twelve verses, or one hundred and ninety-three words, while Luke and Mark content themselves with scarcely more than one-third of that amount. But are we warranted in supposing, much less in confidently affirming (as we must do to find a discrepancy), that the admonitions of Christ on that occasion were no more extended and particular and personal than they appear to be from

[1] See Geikie's Life of Christ, Vol. II. p. 643.

these reports? As far as possible from it. On the contrary, we have every reason to believe that at such a crisis of their history there would have been a prolonged conversation between Christ and his disciples. How dangerous it is to draw inferences from negative testimony in such a case, is illustrated in the reports given by the evangelists of the last interview between Christ and his disciples before his arrest. Had the accounts of Matthew, Mark, and Luke alone been left us, we should have known even less of what occurred on that memorable occasion than we now do of the conversation which took place when the apostles first received their commission, and were sent out on their trial journey. But John has also left an account of the last interview before the arrest, and nearly five chapters[1] are occupied with reporting the words of Jesus upon that occasion.

112. From this we see how little warrant any one can have for narrowing down the discourse of Christ upon the important occasion of inducting the apostles into their office to the one hundred and ninety-three words recorded by Matthew. Now it cannot be denied that the impression made upon the mind by these three accounts is essentially the same; and a little attention will show that the apparent discrepancies can easily enough be accounted for, even on the theory of verbal

[1] John xiii.-xvii.

inspiration. To bring about this harmony we need only suppose that Christ's whole discourse occupied a half hour, and consisted of five hundred words. The common impression made by each one of the accounts is, that the disciples were to be lightly attired, free from care, and wholly devoted to their work. Any one familiar with the bold and powerful antitheses of the Sermon on the Mount will not be troubled with finding in one part of the Saviour's discourse, on such an occasion, the command to "take *no* staff," and in another part, to "take *only* a staff." Every word can come in easily and harmoniously enough when, by a proper use of the historic imagination, the whole scene is brought to view. Suppose, as the Saviour was proceeding, his eye fell on a poor disciple whose entire outfit consisted of a staff, a wallet, sandals, and a single tunic; that would naturally give a turn to the portion of the discourse related by Mark; and with his eye fixed on him, Christ would naturally say: "Take [αἴρωσιν] nothing for your journey, save a staff only; no bread, no wallet, no money in your purse; but go shod with sandals, and do not put on two coats." His eye falling on another who has not even a staff, he says, as reported by Matthew and Luke: "Go forth just as you are; get [κτήσησθε] you no gold, nor silver, nor brass in your purses; no wallet for your journey, neither two coats, nor shoes, nor staff." It is utterly immaterial whether you take a staff or not, but go forth devoted entirely to your spiritual mission. This is the true inference respecting the passage, rather than the conclusion of Dr. Ladd that "the detail as to *two* tunics was impressed indelibly, while the command as to the staff was indefinite in their minds."[1]

113. It is equally easy to dispose of what is said about the impossibility of harmonizing the two reports of the Sermon on the Mount. But here, again, we find Dr. Ladd declaring that they "are so essentially two different, and in some respects discrepant, accounts that no harmony is possible."[2] These reports are found in Matt. v., vi., and vii., and Luke vi. 17-49. That they are reports of two different discourses is *possible;* in which case there will be no occasion to consider the alleged discrepancies. But that they are reports of one discourse is *probable* from the extended and striking resemblances of the two. "The beginning and ending of both are the same; there is a general similarity in the order and often identity in the expressions."[3] But, in considering the possibility of harmonizing the two accounts, we should consider how brief they both are, even though long in

---

[1] Vol. I. pp. 400, 401.
[2] Ibid., p. 402.
[3] Andrews' Life of Our Lord, p. 252.

comparison with the ordinary reports of the Saviour's addresses. Matthew's report of the sermon is comprised in one hundred and seven verses, while Luke's contains only thirty. Probably, however, even Matthew's account is not one-fourth part of the whole sermon of our Lord, adapted as it was in extemporaneous discourse to the varied wants of the vast multitude.

114. The apparent difference in *time* may arise from the fact that Matthew does not connect his facts in chronological order — a thing which, as a historian, he was under no obligation to do, unless that was his professed object. As to the apparent discrepancy in the *place* in which the sermon is said to have been preached, it is sufficient to remark that where the description of the movements of a great multitude at such an exciting time is compressed by one evangelist into a single verse, and is expanded by another into only four verses, there is little reason to expect minuteness of topographical description. A mountain occupies a large territory; and when Matthew simply says that "Jesus went up into a mountain, and when he was set his disciples came unto him; and he opened his mouth and taught them," he has in no way or manner contradicted the more minute account of Luke, who says he came down into a level place (τόπου πεδινοῦ). Level places may be numerous on the sides of a mountain.

115. It is needless to deny that many attempts to harmonize the Gospel narratives have been unnecessarily extravagant and fanciful. Nevertheless, the fact remains that, after careful study of the subject, the great mass of sober-minded scholars have been satisfied that there is no occasion to ascribe inaccuracy even in details to any one of the evangelists. The burden of proof rests upon those who allege the inaccuracies; and so many of their cases have been explained in the processes of modern investigation that this burden of proof is growing continually heavier. The renewed charges of inaccuracy brought from time to time against the Bible are not made necessary by the discovery of new facts. They are rather the result either of the imperfect acquaintance of new authors with the discussions that have gone before, or of a failure properly to appreciate the supernatural character of Christianity, which makes many things probable that would not otherwise be so.

XI.

ALLEGED ERRORS OF THE NEW TESTAMENT IN QUOTING THE OLD.

116. In many cases of quotation from the Old Testament, and of references to its facts, the writers of the New Testament are said to take a liberty with the Old which is inconsistent with the theory that the Old Testament is inspired in all its parts. In other cases it is alleged that the writers of the New Testament misapprehend and misapply the prophecies of the Old Testament, or even distort its facts. In considering some of these alleged discrepancies it seems best, as in the previous section, to begin with such as have been made prominent by recent writers. Dr. Ladd again makes this class of objections the basis of his criticisms upon the ordinary view of inspiration.

The first case to which we allude is too trivial to have deserved attention but for the prominence given it by Dr. Ladd; yet its triviality will not prevent its serving to illustrate a principle. Matt. xxiv. 37 sq. reports Christ as saying that in the "days which were before the flood they were eating and drinking, marrying and giving in marriage, until the day that Noah entered into the ark." Professor Ladd sees here indications that Christ was "following a tradition of the flood which differed in some particulars from that of the Hebrew Scriptures"; and he calls upon the reader to "notice the features added to the narrative of Genesis; especially the word πίνοντες [drinking] in apparent contradiction of the narrative of Gen. ix. 20."[1] How little the occasion to find a discrepancy here will appear when the passage referred to in Genesis is quoted: "And Noah began to be an husbandman, and he planted a vineyard, and drank of the wine, and was drunken."[2] How any one should infer from this passage in Genesis that there was no drinking before the flood it is difficult to imagine; for the phrase "'began to be an husbandman' cannot mean that this was the first time he had practised husbandry, but the beginning of it after the flood."[3]

117. Dr. Ladd also thinks that in Christ's reference[4] to the famine in the time of Elijah,[5] "he seems to incorporate that divergent Jewish tradition which extended the duration of the drought to three years and a half, and which James also ac-

---

[1] Ladd, as above. Foot note on page 69.
[2] Gen. ix. 20, 21.
[3] Tayler Lewis on Genesis in Lange's Commentary.
[4] Luke iv. 25–27.
[5] 1 Kings xvii. 9 ff.

cepts, and employs the popular hyperbole which spoke of the drought as extending over the whole earth."[1] Now the whole of this reference to "divergent Jewish tradition" and "popular hyperbole" in this case is purely imaginary and gratuitous. One has but to consult the Greek lexicon, or, for that matter, the Revised Version of 1881, or even that of 1611, to see that Christ did not say over the whole *earth*, but over the whole *land*, this being a perfectly allowable translation for the Greek word γῆ *(gee)*; and in James the presence of hyperbole is even less manifest, since the word "whole" is absent. As to extending the drought to three years and a half, there is nothing to prevent such an extension, since in Kings it is simply said: "There shall not be dew nor rain these years,"[2] and at the command of the Lord Elijah went up to the brook Cherith, and remained until the brook dried up, which is said to have been "after a while"; whereupon the Lord commanded the prophet to go to Zarephath; "and it came to pass, after many days, that the word of the Lord came to Elijah in the third year, saying, Go, shew thyself unto Ahab; and I will send rain upon the earth."[3] It is not said that this is the third year of the famine, but the more natural inference is that it is the third year of his stay at Zarephath, which with the "after a while" would make the whole

---

[1] Vol. I. p. 69.   [2] 1 Kings xvii. 1.   [3] 1 Kings xviii. 1.

time neither very much more nor very much less than three years and six months. Instead of drawing from this instance, as Dr. Ladd does, the inference that Christ "thus manifests his entirely uncritical attitude towards the details of the narrative,"[1] the extreme advocates of verbal inspiration might infer that Christ's attitude was intended to be very critical, and that he intended to give the weight of his authority to a minutely accurate interpretation of the Old Testament account.

118. Another case introduced by Dr. Ladd will lead the way to some additional remarks concerning the correct view of the relation of words to things, and enable us to clear away some prevalent misconceptions as to the functions of language. Isa. xxix. 13 contains a somewhat obscure sentence, translated in our version, "And their fear toward me is taught by the precept of men" (literally, from the Hebrew, "And their fear toward me has become a precept of men, taught"). Christ, in quoting this, follows very closely the translation of the Septuagint: "But in vain do they worship me, teaching *as their* doctrines the precepts of men."[2] Upon this, Professor Ladd has to remark that Christ follows the Septuagint "in introducing the important word μάτην [in vain], which has no correlative in the Hebrew text. This is done apparently to justify his application of the

---

[1] Vol. I. p. 69.   [2] Matt. xv. 9.

prophecy as περὶ ὑμῶν [concerning you]."[1] Now, it is indeed true, as Professor Ladd says, that there is no single word here in the Hebrew corresponding to "in vain"; but in transferring thought from one language to another the translator could make little progress if he were compelled to use only such words as were exactly correlative. The thought of a writer cannot be obtained by pulverizing his sentences and subjecting the product to chemical analysis. The thought of a sentence is largely conveyed by the collocation of the words and by paying due regard to usages of speech for which we can give no reason. A particular thought is often held in a sentence in solution, as sugar is in water, and crystallizes into a word only when subjected to the process of translation, — a process which is, in many respects, like that of evaporation from one liquid and resolution in another. In the present case, the "in vain" of the Septuagint is *im*plicitly in the Hebrew sentence, and it falls within the proper province of a translation to bring it out *ex*plicitly in Greek. To serve God merely in obedience to human authority is to entirely miss the end of worship, and is utterly in vain. We surely should be willing to grant the writers of the New Testament the liberties of an ordinary translator. In transferring the thought of the

[1] Vol. I. p. 71.

ALLEGED ERRORS IN QUOTATION. 189

Hebrew into Greek forms even a paraphrase may be necessary.

119. The Book of Hebrews has been specially discredited by some on account of the character of its Old Testament quotations, Professor Toy even affirming that "it shows an entire disregard of the connection of thought of the Old Testament," and that it cites "from it a passage which is not found in the Hebrew," "and in one passage reverses the sense of the original."[1]

The passage which it is alleged is not found in the Hebrew is Heb. i. 6, "And let all the angels of God worship him." An examination of the facts, however, will show that Professor Toy's confident assertion is far from being correct. There are two places in the Old Testament where the Septuagint has a clause equivalent to that in Hebrews; viz. Deut. xxxii. 43 and Ps. xcvii. 7, Deuteronomy reading, "Let all the angels of God worship him," and Psalms, "Worship him, all ye his angels." In Deuteronomy there is nothing in the Hebrew which can be construed as an equivalent of the clause; but in Psalms there is, the passage reading literally, "Worship him, all ye gods." Before Professor Toy is warranted in his sweeping assertion, therefore, he is bound to consider the question, whether the Hebrew word translated "gods" (אֱלֹהִים) is not sufficiently elastic to per-

[1] Quotations in the New Testament, p. xxxvii.

mit it to be translated "angels" in some connections. Following the assertion of Gesenius, Professor Toy affirms that אֱלֹהִים never means "angels." But upon this we join issue with him, and affirm that no one knows enough about Hebrew usage to be so confident as he is in his affirmation. In the first place, it should count for something that the scholars who translated the Septuagint understood אֱלֹהִים to mean "angels" both here and in the eighth Psalm, where the clause "Thou hast made him a little lower than the angels" might read in Hebrew "a little lower than God." In the second place, it should count for something, also, that in both these cases the author of the Book of Hebrews endorses the translation of the Septuagint. In the third place, the elasticity of the word אֱלֹהִים appears in Ps. lxxxii. 6, where the *judges* of Israel are addressed as "gods" (אֱלֹהִים); and in John x. 35 Christ himself endorses that use of the word. From all this it appears that "divine-like honor and dignity, therefore, are all that, in such cases, can be fairly understood by the term. And as the angels stand highest in this respect among created intelligences known to men, they are not unnaturally regarded as the beings that most fully answer to the description. Substantially, therefore, the Greek version here gives the sense of the original; and some of the best commentators still concur in it as the most appropriate rendering that can be given."¹

120. Professor Toy's assertion that in Heb. x. 5–10 the quotation from the Old Testament "reverses the sense of the original," deserves attention both from the confidence with which it is put forth and from the intrinsic difficulty of the passage. But here, also, the question is not regarding a fact which is fully ascertained, but whether Professor Toy properly understands the fact. Whether the sense of the original is reversed by the author of Hebrews or not, depends upon the interpretation of the passage. The passage reads: [5] "Wherefore when he cometh into the world, he saith, Sacrifice and offering thou wouldest not, but a body didst thou prepare for me; [6] in whole burnt offerings and *sacrifices* for sin thou hadst no pleasure: [7] then said I, Lo, I am come (in the roll of the book it is written of me) to do thy will, O God. [8] Saying above, sacrifices and offerings and whole burnt offerings and *sacrifices* for sin thou wouldest not, neither hadst pleasure therein (the which are offered according to the law), [9] then hath he said, Lo, I am come to do thy will. He taketh away the first, that he may establish the second. [10] By which will we have been sanctified through the offering of the body of Jesus Christ once for all." The clause in the fifth verse,

---
¹ Fairbairn's Hermeneutical Manual, p. 444.

"a body didst thou prepare for me," appears to have no corresponding clause in Ps. xl. 6–8, from which the quotation is made. But to say that it "reverses the sense of the original" is incorrect. The phrase in Ps. xl. 6 corresponding to "a body thou hast prepared for me," is "My ears hast thou opened," which is probably a figurative way of saying, "Thou hast made me obedient," which, under another figure, may also be taken as the sense of the clause, "a body thou hast prepared for me." "The implication of the phrase [a body thou hast prepared for me] σῶμα κατηρτίσω μοι, in the connection where it stands, is, that this body was to be a victim instead of the legal sacrifices; of course *a devotedness of the highest nature* is implied. *Ad sensum*, then, in a general point of view, the text may be regarded as cited; and this, oftentimes, is all at which the New Testament writers aim."[1]

121. The scope of the present brief treatise will not permit us to examine in detail all of the instances in which the writers of the New Testament are alleged to have misunderstood or to have misquoted the Old Testament. Our object here is to illustrate the principles upon which those apparent misapplications are to be explained. A number of instances were considered by way of illustration in the chapter treating of the Interpretation of

[1] Stuart's Commentary on Hebrews, p. 552.

ALLEGED ERRORS IN QUOTATION. 193

Scripture. For examination of all the cases in detail, the reader is referred to special treatises upon the subject.[1] It should be remembered, however, that in the majority of cases where the Old Testament is quoted by the writers of the New, there is no seeming difficulty to one who admits the supernatural character of Christianity, and who will grant to Christ and the apostles in interpreting the Old Testament a small portion of the authority which is claimed by modern commentators. Professor Fairbairn at the close of his patient examination of such cases gives the following general result:[2] Of the one hundred and thirty-six quotations of the Old Testament in the New considered (which, not reckoning the repeated citations, include all that are really formal citations), seventy-two correspond exactly with the Hebrew, thirty differ from it in points so slight as to indicate no diversity of sense, seventeen follow the Septuagint where it seems to diverge to some extent from the Hebrew; but "the variations are commonly of a formal kind; and even when they exhibit a substantial difference, it is only by a sort of paraphrastic explanation being given of the original, or by a distinct impression being imparted

[1] Haley's Alleged Discrepancies of the Bible; Fairbairn's Hermeneutical Manual, pp. 390-503; Davidson on Sacred Hermeneutics, pp. 334-515; Horne's Introduction, Vol. II. pp. 113-207; Tholuck in *Bibliotheca Sacra*, Vol. xi. pp. 568-616.
[2] Hermeneutical Manual, p. 452.

to a particular aspect of the truth, such as specifying a result or a cause, which the original did nothing more than indicate. In none of the cases are we presented with a different sense, but simply with a modified representation of the same sense. And in the remaining seventeen, in which neither is the Hebrew nor the Septuagint strictly followed, there is a common principle pervading them;[1] that, namely, of rendering something peculiar or obscure in the original more clearly intelligible to those who were immediately in the eye of the New Testament writer, or to readers generally in gospel times. In the whole of this class of cases, as well as of the immediately preceding one, the general meaning of the ancient Scripture is still preserved, and nothing in doctrine or precept is built upon the superficial differences existing between the citation and the original."

[1] The Hebrew was not a spoken language in the time of Christ, but was represented by the dialect formerly known as Chaldee, now known as Aramaic. There are many indications, besides this last class of quotations referred to, which indicate that in the time of Christ there was a popular translation in the Aramaic language of the Hebrew Bible. See Prof. Böhl's "Forschungen nach einer Volksbibel zur Zeit Jesu."

XII.

HARMONY OF THE BIBLE WITH SCIENCE.

122. At this point it is proper to make a few remarks upon the alleged contradictions between the Bible and science, most prominent of which are those between Genesis and geology and between the Bible and the supposed teachings of science concerning the antiquity of man. Upon each of these topics it is important to notice that before a conflict can be established we must be sure that we have properly interpreted the facts both of science and the Bible. Few, however, would now be disposed to deny that geology teaches that the world was created countless ages ago, and that the separate epochs of creation were not days of twenty-four hours each. This would therefore bring the scientific man in conflict with Moses if we are shut up to a mechanical and inelastic interpretation of the inspired words in the first chapter of Genesis. But we are not thus shut up. There are two very plausible lines of interpretation (each depending on the well-known elasticity of the word "day") which keep clear of

conflict with modern scientific investigations. The word day, as every one knows, has a great variety of significations. For example, if in the first chapter of Genesis "day" means twenty-four hours, and seven such days are indicated, what should we say of Gen. ii. 4, which speaks of the whole work having been done in one day ("These *are* the generations of the heavens and of the earth when they were created, in the day that the Lord God made the earth and the heavens")? and what shall we say of Deut. ix. 1, where Moses tells the people that they shall pass over Jordan this day, while knowing well that they should not do so until after his death? The elasticity of the word is also seen at once in such a phrase as "This will not happen in your day," where a very indefinite period is meant. We might even say, "Rome, in the day of her power, was mistress of the world," when the word would cover a considerable period. Proceeding from this range in the use of the word day, some fail to see any reference here to periods of time at all, and would say, "The object of Moses in the first chapter of Genesis is so evidently to counteract the polytheism of his day, and to assert the monotheism which is so characteristic a doctrine of Jewish belief, that it could not have been in his mind to make prominent the petty details of scientific discovery relating to the time and mode of creation.

But he contents himself with affirming in sublimest forms of speech that God is the Creator of all things. This he does both in general and in detail, — grouping together under the work of the several days the whole list of objects to which idolatrous worship was paid, and affirming that they were all nothing but created objects, and that man was in dignity higher than all other created things, and hence it was very foolish to worship them."[1]

123. Another view, however, has been entertained in recent times by many eminent scientific men. This view regards the six days of creation mentioned by Moses as six great periods or cosmogonic days, which are supposed to have marked the progress of the earth's creation up to the advent of man;[2] and it certainly is a most remarkable occurrence that centuries before the Christian era an orderly account of creation should have been written into which it is so easy to adjust all the facts of modern science. Even the theories of evolution, so far as they are capable of proof, find little to oppose them in this remarkable composition. As Professor Guyot has pointed out, the language of Genesis would necessitate only three distinct periods of creation, leaving the

[1] See these views more fully developed in the author's Studies in Science and Religion, Chap. vii.
[2] See especially Creation, or the Biblical Cosmogony in the Light of Modern Science, by Arnold Guyot, one of the latest and most consistent interpreters of this theory.

rest to proceed by natural processes. It is a fact not-sufficiently observed, that there are two words in Genesis to represent the act of creation; namely, *bará* and *asáh* (בָּרָא and עָשָׂה), of which *bará* (to create) is used only when speaking of the first creation of the heavens and the earth (verse 1), of the creation of animals (verse 21), and of the creation of man (verse 27); elsewhere, the less specific word *asáh* (to make) is used, or even more ambiguous forms of expression like "Let the waters bring forth" (verse 20), which positively favors some form of evolution. From this the distinguished authority whose views we are considering, infers that absolute creation is affirmed in Genesis only at three stages; namely, the beginning of the universe, the beginning of life, and the beginning of man,—precisely the three places where all theories of evolution completely and hopelessly break down in their evidence. Thus, according to our author, "the question of evolution within each of these great systems—of matter into various forms of matter, of life into the various forms of life, and of mankind in all its varieties—remains still open."[1]

124. On either of these theories of the interpretation of the first chapter of Genesis, it certainly is a marvellous result that a cosmogony should have been presented at that early day in

[1] Creation, p. 128.

language that can be easily interpreted so as to avoid conflict with the science of the present day. No other religious system has a cosmogony with which the men of science can by any possibility be at peace.

So far, then, from finding anything in the cosmogony of Genesis to bear against the inspiration of the Bible, we may draw from it a powerful argument in favor of inspiration. In the words of another, "On any other hypothesis than that of divine inspiration, this first chapter of Genesis, and in particular this account of the fifth and sixth days of creation, is the most unaccountable production ever written by the pen of man. Consider by whom this chapter was written. It was written by a man who lived far back in the early infancy of human knowledge — a man who had not, and could not have, any knowledge whatever, any least conception or suspicion, of the actual reality of the vast development of which he was telling the story. And yet of that development, going on through countless ages, he has followed the order of events in a full and comprehensive outline — an outline so true and exact that not one mistake or defect can be pointed out in it from beginning to end. How could such a thing be? How did this man know that a robe of waters covered the earth before a ray of light from the sun had penetrated to its surface? How did this man know that the enormous vegetation of the coal period had flourished two and three of the great creative days before the higher animals were called into being? How did he know that it was not until the fourth day that the sun shone clearly upon the earth? How did he know that fish of every kind, gigantic reptiles, and birds, filled the earth on the fifth day; while the mammalia and man, the crown of all, were not called into being until the sixth day, at the very close of the long creative work? Clearly he wrote better than he knew. Some vision of the grand evolution of material things passed before his mental eye; and the story of creation as he thus saw it he has told. Science examines this story and finds it true and exact in every point. What shall we say of a record like this, dating back to the very childhood of our race, yet so strangely anticipating the maturest results of scientific investigation? There is but one thing which can be said,—a judgment which we are compelled to repeat with every new examination of the sacred volume,—'All Scripture is given by inspiration of God.'"[1]

125. The alleged conflict between the chronology of the Bible and that of modern archæology is likewise dependent upon two uncertain elements: *a*. Does the Bible teach that the human race has been upon the earth only about six thousand

[1] Fundamental Questions, by Edson L. Clark, pp. 26, 27.

years? or, indeed, does it contain any definite system of chronology? *b.* Have archæologists proved a very great antiquity to the human race? To the first of these questions, whether the Bible is explicitly committed to a short system of chronology for the human race, we think that an unprejudiced examination must answer in the negative. It should be remembered that the chronological figures in the margins of our reference Bibles were not prepared by an inspired writer, but by Archbishop Usher, whose chronological scheme has by no means a clear field, but is one of nearly two hundred schemes drawn up from the fragmentary data of the Bible. It is easily seen, even in some of the most formal genealogies of the Bible, that the main object of the writer was not to furnish a complete and accurate chronology, but rather to indicate lines of descent and facts of relationship. For example, in the genealogy of Christ as given in Matt. i. 1–17, the writer doubtless knew that many links were omitted; as where it is said that "Joram begat Ozias" (verse 8); whereas, if every link had been given according to 1 Chron. iii. 11, 12, it would have read "Joram begat Ahaziah, Ahaziah begat Joash, Joash begat Amaziah, and Amaziah begat Ozias." A still more instructive case occurs in Ezra, where Azariah is called the "son of Meraioth," and this in a genealogical table; whereas, according to 1 Chron. vi. 7–11, Azariah was the sixth generation from Meraioth. Again, in 1 Chron. xxvi. 24, we read: "Shebuel the son of Gershom, the son of Moses, was ruler of the treasures." This was in David's time, several hundred years after Moses. Yet Gershom was the son of Moses, while Shebuel was twelve or fifteen generations from the person whose son he is said to be; and this the writer, and those for whom he wrote, must have known.[1]

From this it is plain that the Jews, like other oriental nations, introduced their genealogical tables not so much to furnish an accurate chronology in years as to emphasize the fact of lineal descent and consanguinity; so that we even find it said in Gen. x. 15-18 that Canaan begat not only two individuals that are mentioned, but also nine tribes or nations which are specified! Such are the indefinite materials from which the so-called systems of biblical chronology are made out. From which it is clear that chronology was not one of the things which the Bible set out to teach, but that the sacred writers have left the subject so open that it will be very difficult for archæologists to come into collision with the general chronological statements of the Scripture, even if it should be proved that the human race had been in the world a great many thousand years.

[1] See the author's Studies in Science and Religion, pp. 371-377.

126. And, on the other hand, the enormous antiquity claimed for the human race by some writers on archæology is far from being an established fact. It still remains true that the historical monuments of Egypt and Assyria cannot be proved to be more than five thousand years old; and the evidences of palæolithic man, which are the earliest vestiges of the human race yet discovered or likely to be discovered, and which probably, both in Europe and America, antedate the close of the glacial period, are by no means so ancient as some have supposed. Indeed, evidence of great force is accumulating to show that the ice of the glacial period did not withdraw from the northern part of the United States at a period much more than eight thousand years ago.[1]

Thus it appears that, come what may, the chronology of the Bible and the chronology of the archæologists will have little difficulty in adjusting themselves to each other, for that of the Bible can easily be lengthened out to meet any demands which archæology is likely to make upon it. And here, again, in this freedom from positive statements upon unessential points — so characteristic of the Bible — we find evidence of a guiding and restraining hand that we cannot be amiss in believing to be divine.

[1] See an article by the author on The Niagara Gorge as a Chronometer in the *Bibliotheca Sacra*, vol. xli. pp. 369-376; also Chap. vi. in Studies in Science and Religion.

XIII.

PORTIONS OF SCRIPTURE SAID TO BE INSIGNIFICANT OR UNWORTHY OF INSPIRATION.

127. REFERENCE has already been made [1] to the similarity between the criticisms upon the doctrine of design in nature and those upon the doctrine of inspiration in Scripture. In nature, as in Scripture, there are many things which seem too insignificant to be ascribed to the agency of God. For example, in the most perfect animals there are many rudimentary and apparently useless parts. The whale has seven vertebræ in his neck, so thin and compressed that a single vertebra would seem to have been sufficient. The young calf has teeth in the front part of his upper jaw which never cut through the gums. The horse has several bones about his ankle that seem to serve no purpose, but are rather an encumbrance and an occasion of disease. The vermiform appendix is in man an extension of the large intestine for which physiologists can see no use; but, on the other hand, it is frequently the occasion of disease and death.

[1] Paragraph 68.

In the vegetable world there are innumerable phenomena to which we can ascribe no purpose, except by falling back upon principles of faith. The pollen annually produced by pine-grains and willow trees, and the spores continually thrown off from fungi and other very low organisms, are well-nigh innumerable, and immensely beyond all ordinary demand; and so of seeds in general. Though apparently every seed is designed for growth, yet myriads upon myriads annually perish where one finds its way to conditions favorable to growth. A large class of writers at the present day criticise nature on account of this waste, and affirm that such waste cannot be an element of design. The brief answer to such objections is, that the designs of God in nature are too comprehensive and complex for man to compass them in their entirety. Yet so much purpose is apparent in nature that it is very unreasonable for the human mind to deny design in the obscure portions of nature, since perhaps they seem obscure only because man is both so limited in his natural capacities and so immature in his development, that his intellectual vision does not penetrate many regions of thought which are still open to higher intelligences, and may at some time be open to him. It is the part of human wisdom to take a low place among the critics of the divine workmanship. Nature is designed as a whole, and the perfection of its parts is not absolute, but relative.[1] That which is perfection in the pollen of the pine-tree is not the perfection pertaining to the pollen of an orchid; for in each case there is a correlation between the quantity of pollen produced and the means by which it is transported to its place of fertilization. In one case the wind is depended upon to transport it, and the pollen grains have to be more numerous than the chances of failure, in order to secure the proper amount of fertilization. In seeds, also, which are dependent upon natural agencies for transportation, there is endless diversity in the means provided. Evidently it is the Creator's design that many troublesome weeds should have great facility of self-propagation. The thistle is provided with a downy tuft of sufficient levity to float the seed in the air, and avail itself of wind-transportation. Burrs of various kinds are specially adapted to adhere to the feathers of birds, the fur and wool of animals, and thereby to avail themselves of every method of animal transportation. Thus seeds are transported with costly furs, along all the lines of traffic through which flows the commerce of the Hudson's Bay Company. Thus, also, the wool merchant is the means of transporting to England and France seeds native to California, Australia, and South America.

[1] See the author's Studies in Science and Religion, pp. 165-255.

128. We are not permitted to judge of the design of any minute portion of nature by the part it seems to us to play at the present moment. Nature is a vast storehouse of divine adaptation designed for all time. The naturalist now sees in the numerous rudimentary organs to which we have already called attention striking marks of design directly operative in the past; and these marks are still of inestimable value to the human mind as indexes which reveal the handiwork of God in former times. Nor do we know the exigencies of the future sufficiently to affirm with confidence that every appendage which now seems to be useless must always be useless. We are bound to reason about the plans of God as we would about the plans of a far-seeing statesman. He would be foolish indeed who in time of profound peace should decide that all the preparations of the navy-yard and arsenal were superfluous.

129. In criticising particular portions of the Bible we are bound to consider the complexity of the service the Bible is designed to render. The Bible is like a ship making a long voyage, passing alternately from temperate zone to torrid, and thence through temperate to frigid, and back again. In judging of the wisdom of each particular portion of its outfit, all the vicissitudes of the voyage must be taken into account. The wisdom of the ship-builder is not alone seen in the flying pennants and

the figure-head, but also in the various internal arrangements giving strength and capacity to the vessel, and providing for the convenience, health, and comfort of the passengers and crew. Viewed from this aspect, it will be found difficult to prove that any portions of the Bible are either unnecessary or unworthy. If the Bible was to be adapted to human wants, it must have a human side complete and perfect. It is by the complete incorporation of all human methods of expressing truth that the Bible is made an intelligible and adequate revelation of the divine will; and to criticise the Bible, because it employs every device of language and literature by which truth is conveyed from one mind to another, is to hoist ourselves with our own petard, and to reveal the fallibility of our own logic rather than the imperfection of the Bible.

130. Under this head it is proper to remark upon various alleged literary infelicities of Scripture which in many cases are thought even to obscure its meaning. For example, much of the teaching of the Bible is indirect, — a principle being taught not by plain precept, but by an illustration or an example in which we are simply aided to the discovery of the specific course of duty by considering the example in the light of our own reason and experience. It is thus that we have been left to learn the full extent of the evils of slavery and of the use of alcoholic bever-

ages. A little attention shows, however, that the relations of life are so complex that it is difficult to state many of the rules of conduct in anything more than a general form; and it is impossible to embody the principles of divine action in any single statement which shall not be liable to misunderstanding.

For example, the teaching of the Book of Job is not wholly contained in the words ascribed to the Lord, but the signification and effect of these divine words depend in great measure upon the discordant dialogue of uninspired men which has preceded. The preacher would indeed make a grave mistake if he quoted the words of Bildad or of Satan as if they in themselves contained the truth of God. But being professedly put in the mouths of persons whose character is known, their relation to the whole book becomes evident enough, — they are the intensified darkness of the background from which streams the light of God; they are the temporary notes of discord out of which by the divine touch arises the celestial harmony of the whole.

131. It is somewhat thus that we may regard a large portion of the Book of Proverbs. Some of the proverbs are said to be below the standard of the ordinary wise sayings of the East. It should be remembered, however, that we cannot judge the separate portions of the book apart from the

whole, but must remember that, like the body spoken of by Paul, a collection of wise sayings has many members, and those members which seem to be more feeble may yet be necessary. The eyes may be more honorable in themselves than the finger nails. Nevertheless, we are better off with two eyes and ten perfect fingers than we should be with a dozen eyes and a supply of imperfect fingers. It is not perfection in literature to have every sentence striking and brilliant. Let any one attempt to eliminate from the Book of Proverbs the portions sometimes said to be of inferior worth, and he will find that his selection of choice proverbs will not be read and enjoyed as much as the whole book is now. Too much sweetness may cloy the appetite. Too much brightness dazzles the vision. We may readily admit all that is said about the inferiority in some respects, of the Book of Esther to Pilgrim's Progress, or of Solomon's Songs to the Westminster Catechism, and yet maintain that both Esther and Solomon's Songs may be perfectly fitted to complete the circle of literary impression which a divine written revelation needed to make; whereas, neither of those valuable human productions would serve the purpose. There is doubtless a greater range of truth in Baxter's Saints' Rest than in the Book of Ecclesiastes; but Baxter's light is borrowed light, while Ecclesiastes belongs to the self-luminous constellations of the sky.

132. Among the trifling matters sometimes spoken of as unworthy of being regarded as the products of inspiration, are such incidents as Paul's directing Timothy to bring with him the cloak that he left at Troas with Carpus, and the books, especially the parchments;[1] and his advice to Timothy to drink no longer water, but a little wine for his stomach's sake and often infirmities.[2] Such objectors forget how largely human life is made up of small things, and of how much our comfort depends upon attention to them. A revelation from God that did not come in human costume, and that was not penetrated with the spirit of human sympathy, would be ill adapted to its purpose, and would be like a Saviour who should have come neither eating nor drinking, and subject to no ordinary temptations. But as it behooved Christ to take upon him not the form of angels, but of the sons of Abraham, and to be tempted in all respects as we are, yet without sin; so it behooves the divine revelation to be altogether human in its form, except that it give no positive countenance to error. Even as a matter of literature, Paul's request for the cloak is a most effective means of revealing to us the hardships and the haste of his laborious ministry. His heart was burdened with

---

[1] 2 Tim. iv. 13. [2] 1 Tim. v. 23.

sympathy for his co-laborers, and he avoided as much as possible being a burden to them. He wrought no miracles for his own advantage, and commended prudence as a virtue. If it is important to have the inner experience of such a man revealed to us at all, it could scarcely be done in a more effective way than by securing a record of these two simple requests.[1]

Nor would we set aside the record in 1 Cor. i. 14–17 as an unworthy product of divine inspiration. [14] "I thank God that I baptized none of you, save Crispus and Gaius; [15] lest any man should say that ye were baptized into my name. [16] And I baptized also the household of Stephanas: besides, I know not whether I baptized any other. [17] For Christ sent me not to baptize, but to preach the gospel: not in wisdom of words, lest the cross of Christ should be made void."

The doctrine of inspiration does not imply that the writers were omniscient, but only that they were divinely guided to the utterance, in the best form, of those moral and religious truths most necessary to the edification of the church and the conversion of the world. Now, with regard to the passage under consideration, By what means, we ask, could the supreme importance of the substance of the gospel above the form be better enforced than by this forgetfulness of the apostle as to whom

[1] See Woods on Inspiration, p. 32.

he had baptized? His forgetfulness of those relatively insignificant facts reveals their relative insignificance.

133. Or, turning to Old Testament history, How is it possible to prove that the story of Jonah is unworthy of the place it has occupied in the religious instruction of Jews and Christians for these more than two thousand years? or to show that there will not be equal need of it for the two thousand years to come? And the moral of the story certainly depends upon its truth. The story of the children who mocked Elisha, and were eaten by bears, is often objected to as unworthy of a place in an inspired record of revelation. Such objectors forget the vast range of influence the Bible is designed to exert. It is sometimes said, that such stories were good for rude and barbarous ages, but the civilized world has long outgrown the need of them. The fact, however, is, that rude and barbarous people are still a vast majority of the world, and every human being is born a barbarian, and passes through a stage of experience when the truth administered through these strange incidents would make but little impression apart from them, or others like them to take their place.

134. It is proper to remark in a similar strain upon the "imprecatory Psalms" and the divine commands for the destruction by Israel of the abominable and besotted native tribes of Canaan.

That these are not mere acts of vindictiveness is evident enough, both from the general forbearance and gentleness of the character of David[1] and of the Mosaic code,[2] and from the recorded delay in the infliction of judgment upon the Amorites, because their cup of iniquity was not yet full.[3] In justification of the exterminating wars of Canaan it is sufficient to observe that they are by divine command, when an imperative necessity existed to keep the chosen people free from contact with the cruel and licentious idolatry of the period; and it is not too much to say that, as a result of this isolation of Israel, and of the abhorrence of idolatry created by it, all those sublime ideas of God's unity and holiness wrought in Jewish history have been preserved which are so indispensable, both to a correct apprehension of Christianity and to the moral progress of the world. Whether we can preserve a sufficiently high ideal of holiness and justice and righteousness without the continual study of these histories may well be questioned. Those who regard these stern facts of Old Testa-

---

[1] 1 Sam. xxiv., xxvi.

[2] The apparent severity of the Mosaic code is simply its faithfulness in the infliction of deserved punishment. For the kindness and consideration shown by it to strangers, see Ex. xii. 49; xxii. 21; xxiii. 9, 12; Lev. xxiv. 22; Num. ix. 14; xv. 15, 16, 29; xxxv. 15; Deut. i. 16; x. 18, 19; xxvi. 12. For the humaneness of the code in general, see an article by Prof. J. B. Sewall in *Bibliotheca Sacra*, Vol. xix. p. 368.

[3] Gen. xv. 16.

ment history as unworthy to be compared with the precepts of Christ, are called upon to show that they can by any other means so effectually keep alive in the world a sense of the true nature of sin as by compelling successive generations to harmonize these facts of Old Testament history with their conceptions of God's nature, character, and responsibilities. We are in constant danger of losing our sense of the personality of God and of the deep-seated guilt of human nature. The destruction of human life by natural forces is not so uncommon an occurrence that we should be startled at the taking of life by divine command; for nature is but God's executioner. It is no uncommon thing for nations and races to pass into decline and utter decay. The volcano, the earthquake, the tornado, and the pestilence annually devour their countless victims. But, though they are really God's messengers, they do not speak to man with a personal voice, and their destruction falls alike upon the evil and upon the good, reminding us rather of the uncertainty of life than of the guilt of individuals. In those vast destructions of human life which follow by natural law in the wake of improvidence and intemperance, their true nature as the retribution of a personal God is disguised under the effects of natural law. But in the destruction of the Canaanites by the command of the Lord, and in the representative utterances of the psalmist when, from the high plane of his sympathy with God in his efforts to bring in the reign of righteousness, he poured out his invectives against the persistent and implacable enemies of God's kingdom, we are brought face to face with the terrible realities of sin. In the ongoings of nature nothing seems so cheap as human life. It may well be doubted if ever there was a better investment made in sacrificing human life than in the wholesale destruction of the antediluvians of Sodom and Gomorrah, of the idolatrous inhabitants of Canaan, and of the forty children [1] whose mocking words at Elisha were an index of the moral condition of the hamlet in which they lived.

We do not say that these things are to be repeated. We acquiesce in them as deeds which we believe to be justified by special divine command in adaptation to peculiar exigencies in human history. As such it is of vital importance to keep hold of them as facts of experience which perpetually warn us that all sinners deserve to perish.

135. It used to be the style to make light of the list of patriarchs and the ethnological tables in Genesis, the minute ceremonial requirements of the Mosaic law, and the genealogical tables of Kings and Chronicles. But now these have become the first portions of the Bible to which

---

[1] The Hebrew word *naar*, however, may mean a full-grown young man, or a servant, or a soldier.

archæologists and antiquarians give attention, and these apparently unworthy parts become the golden hooks in the tabernacle upon which costly curtains are hung;[1] while the repetitions and minutiæ of the Mosaic code seem likely to play a most important part in establishing the historic character of the code itself. We should not lightly cast any part of the Bible aside as of little value. When we attempt to criticise the Bible we are in danger of making the mistake of an unskilled mechanic in criticising a complicated machine. Even an unskilled workman can see that the machine as a whole is wisely designed. But when shown a particular bolt or bar from an obscure portion of the machine he might not discern its use at all. He ought, however, to *believe* that it is of use because of its forming a part of what he knows to be, on the whole, a product of design. The so-called internal evidences of the divine origin of the Bible are not to be applied to its minute portions. We can see the superior excellence of the whole, and on account of that can believe in the excellence of some portions whose function we do not fully comprehend.

[1] Ex. xxvi. 6.

XIV.

CONCLUSION.

136. The method of argument upon which we have depended to prove the divine authority of the Bible is that ordinarily used by natural philosophers in the inductive sciences. In their efforts to discover the laws of nature these philosophers pursue two methods, of which one is called the "method of agreement," the other, the "method of difference." For instance, suppose the problem is to find the immediate cause of the cholera. A large number of cases occur in a great variety of circumstances. One family has the disease while living in a cellar; another, while living in a fashionable house. One person has it who has been careless in his diet; another person has it who has guarded his diet with extreme care. One has it while travelling; another when at home. To determine the real cause of this disease it is necessary to search for that condition which is common to all the cases. The condition of the patients differed in many respects. If that experience can be found in which they agreed before the disease attacked them, some progress will be made toward a determination of the cause of the disease. We have at any rate eliminated from the problem many things which are not causes, and so have narrowed the field of inquiry.

137. But as these cases may have agreed in some unknown respect which was the cause of the disease, the investigator is compelled to employ another process in connection with the foregoing, namely, what is called the "method of difference." He observes the cases of persons whose situation is similar in all respects except that supposed to be the producing cause of the disease and notes if the addition of that one cause uniformly tends to produce the disease, and if the abatement of that cause uniformly tends to a diminution of it.

By properly observing and applying these two rules, one after another of the conditions that have no connection with the production of the disease can be so far eliminated from the problem that at last the exact cause may be determined. Note how these methods apply to the argument for the inspiration of the Bible.

138. Let us first recount the phenomena. The Bible is a sacred book composed of upwards of sixty distinct productions, written by forty or more different writers distributed through a period of about two thousand years. These separate productions comprise almost every kind of literature—

history, biography, poetry, collections of legal maxims and principles, proverbs, hymns, sermons, and prayers, together with extended discussions of the profoundest and most abstruse philosophical questions. These writings were addressed in part to a rude people in rude ages, in part to the most cultivated and philosophic ages and races of the world. The Bible is made attractive to all classes and conditions of men. There is no other book so well calculated as the Bible is to interest and instruct children from generation to generation; and, on the other hand, there is no other book that can so exercise the mind of the philosopher and scholar. The greatest minds the world has ever produced have from time immemorial taxed themselves in vain to fathom the depths of its meaning. The historian, the student of geography and ethnology, the statesman, the poet, find within the lids of the Bible richer mines of wealth in their respective spheres of investigation than any other book affords. When the heart is borne down with sadness and enveloped in the shades of disappointment, there is no language like that of David or Jeremiah with which to give vent to the pent-up feelings. Or when joy and hope thrill the soul, there are none others that can equal Isaiah and the writer of the Revelation in jubilant songs of gladness. But for the Bible there could have been no Hallelujah Chorus.

Such is the diversity apparent in the books of the Bible. Yet amid this diversity there is a most impressive unity. The Bible is not made up of unconnected fragments. There are bricks and mortar and wood and stone. But these are joined together to form one building. There were diverse builders in times far separated, yet they developed one plan. There are foundation, wall, arch, keystone, and spire. The Bible is one as much as St. Peter's church at Rome is one. The Bible, notwithstanding the great variety of authors, is not marred by unnatural excrescences.

139. When the mistakes of transcribers and interpreters have been eliminated from the Bible, it cannot be shown to contain any errors. The Bible endures the searching criticism of this age as no other book does. Its history is unimpeached. None of its numerous geographical references can be proved to be erroneous. Its allusions to manners and customs are without mistake. Its scientific references are made with such caution that it avoids conflict with the discoveries of modern times.

In these respects it differs from other books. There is no other series of histories of one-tenth the compass of the Bible that stands criticism as it does. There is no other sacred book that has kept itself free from conflict with the startling developments of modern science. There is no other book that has grown like the Bible and maintained its symmetry. There is no other book treating of man's relations to God in a manner that has continued to command the respect of men in such diverse conditions and at such widely separated periods.

140. With these facts before us, we seek in the manner of modern philosophers for their producing cause. What has secured this acknowledged and multifarious perfection? What secured the perfection of development manifest in the plan of the Bible in which the law, the history, the rites and ceremonies and liturgies of worship, the prophecies, and the life, death, and doctrines of Christ are indissolubly one? Who fitted the life of Christ into the framework prepared by the Old Testament history? Unaided human agency could not have done it. The arch of unity which the Bible contains stretches across too many centuries, and rises too high, to be the work of man. Look at it. Patchwork shows itself. We might better suppose that St. Peter's at Rome assumed its symmetrical proportions through the unsuperintended work of an army of hod-carriers and stonemasons than to suppose the grand and imposing symmetry of the Bible was the result of the work of forty men laboring, in as many half centuries, without the superintendence of the divine power. Nor is this symmetry of the Bible in all its parts hard to

discover; but it stands out boldly and attracts the notice of all its beholders. Neither does any amount of study dissipate its apparent unity and make it appear an illusion.

141. Again we ask: Who kept forty men in as many half centuries from making any mistakes in historical and geographical references? Does any one say, They kept themselves? But scarcely a single one of other ancient writers is free from mistakes when touching at any length upon these subjects. Why, unless the Holy Spirit granted them aid, should these forty men stand the criticism of modern discoverers better than any other one man who wrote at any length upon similar themes? What kept these forty religious writers, in as many half centuries, from dragging into their books as essential elements of them the crudities of the philosophy and physical science of their times? If history teaches anything it teaches that the temptation for religious founders to dogmatize upon the phenomena of the physical world is well-nigh irresistible. In the light of what other religious founders have done, the chances are a million to one that forty men writing in such diverse periods, would have disfigured their work in a similar manner with crude and silly speculations, had they not been guided by a superior intelligence. Again, What kept these forty writers so uniformly from fulsome flattery of their heroes? They give histories of Abraham, Jacob, David, Solomon, of a long list of kings of Israel and Judah, professedly the chosen instruments of the Lord in developing his plan of redemption; yet they cover up no sin of their heroes — gloss over no baseness of character. What power kept so many writers from flattering royalty, as Virgil flattered Augustus? What restrained the apostles from nonsensical speculations concerning the childhood of Jesus? What kept their records of his miracles from swelling to unnatural proportions? The apocryphal Gospels abound in absurd and silly accounts of Christ's conduct when a child. The miracles alleged to have been performed by certain saints and the shrines of the mediæval church were multiplied to such extent as to rob them of all effect.

We may have fallen into error in some of the minor facts upon which our present conclusion is based, but an error or two where so many facts bear in the same direction would not materially disturb the force of the argument. We are searching for a cause of peculiar phenomena. One factor we know. We know the weakness of man. We know how liable he is to mistakes in geography, history, ethnology, and physical science — how feeble is his grasp of the systems of philosophy which men before him have promulgated. We know how incompetent he is to judge of what is permanent and what is transient in the ideas of his time. We know how easily men are overmastered by the greatness and strangeness of such ideas as form the principal themes of the Bible. From the Talmud and the Targums we know the temptation the Jewish rabbis were under to multiply rules and speculations till their very size should make them unwieldy and useless. From the writings of the Christian commentators on the Bible, — early, mediæval, and modern, — we know how surely man of his own accord loads the truth so heavily with his speculations that it sinks altogether in the sea of forgetfulness. In repeated instances the truth has been so deeply buried beneath frivolous notes, insipid exhortations, fitted at best only for personal and temporal service, that the labor of unearthing it from these voluminous works of the commentators is appalling. Thousands of commentaries have been written on the Book of Romans alone. These characteristic and centrifugal tendencies when operating in the human mind we know. We discover, however, in our Sacred Scriptures evidences of another tendency, revealing the presence of a power from without modifying in a peculiar manner the movements of those minds that wrote the books of the Bible. The problem is to detect and define that power.

142. The astronomers once had a similar problem before them. The motions of the planet

Uranus were found not to conform to the motions which would be produced by the known forces in operation. What effect the attraction of the sun and of the other planets would have upon it could be calculated. But when these had been exhausted there still remained a residuum of effect unaccounted for. From those data the astronomers calculated the size, position, and movements of a planet, exterior to Uranus, whose attraction would explain the irregularities. The telescope was turned in that direction, and the planet revealed itself. Neptune, revolving in an orbit two thousand million of miles distant, was discovered, and the mystery solved. Something such is the problem before us in this discussion. We contemplate in the construction of the Bible the movements not of *one* mind writing on religious subjects, and giving evidence of disturbance or control from without. We have before us not the orbit of *one* planet moving as if in obedience to the attraction of a central sun, but we have *forty* minds in different ages of the world, giving evidence of a uniform control by some external power. We see forty planets moving in well-defined and uniform orbits. Does it need much calculation to assure us that that disturbing power, that attractive force which produces the harmony of movement visible in the sacred writers, is the promised power of God? The enlightened nations of the world continue for the most part to explain the phenomenon upon that theory.

143. This view is rendered almost absolutely certain when we observe that these writers repeatedly affirm that they believe themselves under inspiration of God — a belief which is of itself enough to unbalance any ordinary mind. In this belief we have brought to light a centrifugal force of such strength that, except for the special control of the divine power, it would force the bodies under consideration completely out of their orbits. Forty madmen or impostors or self-deceived teachers could not exhibit such persistent consistency and freedom from error and extravagance on so many points where error and extravagance can easily be detected.

144. Nor is it simply to the providential care displayed in preserving the writers of the Bible from error and extravagance that the appeal is made. There is also a providence manifested in the preservation of the Bible itself. Our English version was translated from an edition of the New Testament that is not now reckoned by any scholars as of much worth in a critical point of view. Modern investigations have brought a flood of light to bear upon the determination of the true text of the Bible since our translation was made. Manuscripts have been gathered and collated from all quarters of the ancient world, and of ages

nearest that of the apostles. Versions that were made into various languages at a very early period have been compared, and single texts that were cited from the Bible by early preachers and writers have been gathered from their voluminous productions. And yet, with all this microscopic examination, there are few material changes to be made in the text from which our translation was rendered, with such integrity has it been handed down to us! The changes made in the revision of the English translation of 1881 cause scarcely a ripple in the discussions of doctrinal theology.

145. Here, we submit, is such a combination of evidences pointing to the divine origin and providential preservation of the Bible as to be absolutely irresistible. In the production and preservation of the Bible we behold the working of a power that far transcends any power of which man alone is capable.

The supposition that God would bestow such care to secure, in the Bible, accuracy of detail and freedom from human extravagances on points where the inaccuracies and extravagances can be tested by us, while allowing its teachings concerning the spiritual world which we have no means of testing to be false, is absurd; for it aims a blow at God's veracity. If God is honest in his dealings with men, he would not impress such manifold and indisputable marks of his care in the minor details of the revelation, and leave the spiritual truth, which we cannot test by scientific means, in ambiguous phrases. These marks of divine care in the production and preservation of the Bible, which we can see and test, are the divine seal upon the whole. They are the superscription of God, certifying that the metal upon which they are impressed is pure gold. We might not be able to test the metal for ourselves, but we can read the superscription — we can recognize the stamp.

146. Thus far we have proceeded in the inductive method of proof. We have examined the things in which we can determine the law of procedure. When we reach the point where our experiment and observation fail, and consider the revelations concerning the eternal world inseparably mingled with all portions of the Bible, shall we say the law abruptly ceases its action, and that God did not continue his supervision further? That would be to say that God cares for the shell, and not for the kernel. That would be to acknowledge that God remembered the hairs of the head and noted the sparrow's fall, but ignored the deepest of all the wants implanted in man's nature. When the inductive reasoner has proved that a law of attraction pervades the solar system, controlling the planets and their satellites, it is not counted credulous to extend the law to the whole material creation. The same imperative duty

rests upon us in our treatment of the Bible. We cannot arbitrarily stop at a certain point, and acknowledge that while a law of providential care has manifestly ruled so far it does not go beyond into fields where we are ignorant. The law being once established by induction we may reason from it deductively. We are not now driven to the necessity of determining the wisdom of each detached doctrine and passage by itself. The evidence that sustains the Scriptures as a whole gives weight to every detached portion. The testimony of Christ and the apostles to the authority of the Old Testament, their acceptance of it as the word of God, in the sense in which the Jews accepted it, is the strongest direct proof we can have of the divine authority of the Old Testament. And the promise to the apostles that the Holy Spirit should speak through them, and the acknowledgment by the apostolic church of the books of the New Testament as of equal authority with the Old Testament, is the most weighty direct testimony we can have that the New Testament is a revelation from God. Each particular part that is proved to be genuine has the weight of authority which is accredited to the whole. As the apostle says: "Every Scripture inspired of God is also profitable for teaching, for reproof, for correction, for instruction which is in righteousness."[1]

[1] 2 Tim. iii. 16.

So far, our argument has been addressed to those who are laboring under doubt, and who are candidly examining the ground on which they are asked to accept the doctrines of the Bible which are beyond the reach of unaided reason — such as, for example, the doctrines of immortality, of prayer, of salvation by Jesus Christ, of the work of the Holy Spirit, and of future retribution. To those who will accept these doctrines, and apply themselves to seek by prayer and faith the experiences which the doctrines profess to confer, the truth may be confirmed by actual experiment. The reasons adduced in the foregoing argument point, like the mathematical calculations of Adams and Leverrier, to an attracting power beyond us. We have but to turn our believing eyes in the direction pointed, and we shall see, as those astronomers saw, the orb itself.

How surpassingly glorious is that orb which the Christian beholds! In spiritual vision he beholds the Son of God! God himself visits the true believer, and consoles and comforts him, and lifts from him the burden of guilt which rested on his conscience. The assurances which the believer possesses of the truth of God's word cannot indeed be directly imparted to others. Nevertheless, this united evidence of the church as to the peculiar joy and satisfaction they find in accepting the teachings of the Scriptures is not without its weight in convincing the world that the Bible is inspired of God. The word of God accomplishes what it promises in this life to the guilty soul that trusts it. This is certainly no small additional evidence that its promises and threatenings respecting the future world are trustworthy.

147. If one is so fortunate as to possess the Bible, his chief work in constructing his religious faith will consist of interpretation. The great question is, "What does the Bible mean?" What prominence is given in it to the various phases of truth? What is the system which underlies its development and teaching? Particular texts are not to be detached from their connection and interpreted as if they stood alone — part is to be compared with part; Scripture is to be understood by Scripture. The Bible is not to be lightly set aside by any one. Its divine sanction claims for it a most exalted place in our affections and study. And the soul may lean upon its promises with unwavering confidence when death draws near, and when all human supports fail. He who builds upon it may fearlessly gaze into the dim vistas of eternity. For God has spoken. In that Word we hear his voice from the darkness, saying, "It is I; peace; be still." Reason and philosophy have no such inspiring and authentic voice.

INDEX.

Accommodation, theory of, 48; not applicable to Christ's endorsement of the Old Testament, 49; nor of Paul's quotations, 117; true, 164sq.; false, 166sq.
Accuracy of the Bible, 221.
Agnosticism, apologetic use of, 130.
Alexandria, catechetical school of, 75.
Alexandrian manuscript, age of, 87.
Analogy between, doctrine of design and of inspiration, 157sq., 204; inspiration and incarnation, 211; Bible and nature, 215.
Analogy of faith, 106, 129.
Antilegomena, 74.
Antiochus Epiphanes, relation of his persecutions to the canon, 69.
Apocalypse of Peter, 75.
Apocalyptic literature, 47.
Apocrypha of the New Testament, 75, 81, 154, 224.
Apocrypha of the Old Testament, books of, enumerated, 47; discarded by Josephus, 64; by Philo, 64; by Origen, 65; by Jerome, 65; by Protestants, 67; seldom quoted by the fathers, 66; Bissell's views of, 66sq.; doctrine and character of, 67, 83.
Apocryphal Gospels, 81.
Apostles, their commission and authority, 18sq., 178; neglect of apocalyptic literature, 47; Teaching of the, referred to, 66; their interpretation of the Old Testament, 110sq.
Apostolic authorship of the New Testament, 82.
Apostolic church, view of, concerning Christ's nature, 121sq.; view of, regarding inspiration, 122sq.; expected the speedy return of Christ, 127.
Aramaic, the language of Christ, 173, 194.
Argument for inspiration, cumulative, 228.
Assimilation, influence of, in producing textual variations, 95sq.

Assyria, chronology of, 203.
Athanasius, canon of the New Testament, 71.
Augustine, on canon of the New Testament, 71.
Authority, divine, claimed for the Bible, 26sq.; by Paul, 26; by Peter, 28; objections to Paul's claim of, 29sq., 211; by the Book of Revelation, 32; by Peter for Paul, 29, 32, 44; thought to be disclaimed by Paul, 29sq.

Bannerman, Professor, quoted, 51, 52.
Barnabas, Epistle of, 75, 81, 155.
Barnabas, miracles of, 23.
Baxter's Saints' Rest, compared with Ecclesiastes, 210.
Beza's manuscript, age of, 87.
Bible, divine authority for the, claimed by Paul, 26; by Peter, 28; the intelligibility of the, 146, 148; Harmony of the, with science, 195-203; chronology of the, indefinite, 201, 202; variety in the, 219; its power to interest, 220; its unity, 221; its accuracy, 221; its unity in diversity, 222sq.; its freedom from error, 222, 227; free from discrepancies, 223, 227; commentaries upon, 225.
Biblical interpretation, 101.
Bissell, Professor E. C., on the Apocrypha, 66sq.
Böhl, Professor, on the Aramaic translation in the time of Christ, 194.
Brevity of the reports of Christ's discourses, 176sq.
Buxtorfs, 161.

Caiaphas, 123.
Calvin as a commentator, 140, 141.
Canaanites, destruction of, 215.
Canon, definition of, 55; relation of the persecutions of Antiochus Epiphanes to the, 69.
Canon of the New Testament, chapter on, 69-84; not dependent

on the action of councils, 69; relation of, to the persecution of Diocletian, 69; Eusebius on, 70; testimony of the second century concerning, 71sq.; of the Syriac Version, 73; of the Muratorian Canon, 73; of the church fathers, 74.
Canon of the Old Testament, chapter on, 55-68; the Jewish, 57; witnessed to by the Book of Ecclesiasticus, 58; by the Apocrypha, 59sq.; by Josephus, 61sq.; by Philo, 64; Melito, 64; Origen, 65; Jerome, 65; the Talmud, 65; the Council of Trent, 67; relation of the persecution of Antiochus Epiphanes to, 69.
Carpzovs, 161.
Cherith, Elijah at, 186.
Christ, supernatural character of, 15sq.; promises inspiration, 18sq.; endorses the Old Testament, 24sq., 56sq.; neglect of apocalyptic literature, 47; did not accommodate the Scriptures, 48sq.; as an interpreter of the Old Testament, 110sq., 114; foreshadowed by types, 111sq.; types referring to, 111sq.; priesthood of, 112; genealogy of, 120, 201; as a teacher, 123sq.; his use of parables, 124, 126; his teachings imperfectly understood by the disciples, 124; his views of the second coming, 130; on demoniacal possession, 168; heals Peter's wife's mother, 171; stills the tempest, 172; and the rich young man, 175; and the Pharisees on divorce, 176.
Christianity, supernatural, 15, 152.
Chronology of the Bible and science, compared, 200-203; indefiniteness of the biblical, 201, 202.
Clark, Edson L., on Genesis and geology, 200sq.
Clement, Epistle of, 75, 155.
Clement of Alexandria on the Book of Hebrews, 75; on Jude, 77; on Second and Third John and Second Peter, 78; on Revelation, 78; quoted Epistle of Barnabas, 81; abounds in quotations from the New Testament, 86; on the New Testament, 154.
Cobbe, Frances Power, quoted, 158.
Comforter, office of the, 19sq.
Commentaries upon the Bible, 225; the newest, not the best, 140.
Consciousness, the ethico-religious, 149.

Conservatism, true, 131.
Context should be considered, 142, 145.
Cook, Canon, on Second Peter, 78sq.
Copernicus, 141.
Cosmogony, biblical, 197.
Cowles, Professor Henry, on Daniel, 113.
Creation, mode of, not asserted in the Bible, 48.
Criticism, Textual, and Inspiration, chapter on, 85-100; necessity for, 85; materials for, 86; quotations and versions, 86, 97, 99; manuscripts, 87; much of it trivial, 88sq., 132, 228; important results of, 91sq., 141; scientific basis of, 94sq.; rules of, 95.
Cross, inscriptions on, 177.
Cumulative argument for inspiration, 228.

Darwinism and Genesis, 198.
Day, meaning of, in Genesis, 196.
Dead, prayers for the, inculcated in the Apocrypha, 67, 83.
Demoniacal possession, 166sq.
Design, full, of an event, sum of all its uses, 118; God's, comprehensive, 158, 205sq.
De Wette, typical character of the Old Testament, 114.
Didymus, on Second Peter, 78.
Difficulties, inherent, 157-170, 204sq.
Diocletian, relation of his persecutions to the canon, 69.
Dionysius of Alexandria on the Revelation of John, 80.
Discrepancies, 121, 134sq.; Alleged verbal, chapter on, 171-183; Bible, free from, 223, 227.
Diseases, mental, 167.
Divorce, 176.
Doctrines, evangelical, 147.
Doketae, view of Christ's nature, 160, 161.

Egypt, chronology of, 203.
Elijah, a type of John the Baptist, 113; during the famine, 185sq.
Elisha and the forty children, 213.
Elohim, meaning of, 121, 190.
Ecclesiastes compared with Baxter's Saints' Rest, 210.
Enoch, Book of, quoted by Jude, 47.
Ephraem manuscript, age of, 87.
Error, alleged, explained, 162, 171sq.; freedom of the Bible from, 222, 227.
Esther compared with Pilgrim's Progress, 210.

Ethico-religious consciousness, 149.
Eusebius, canon of, 70 ; on Epistle of James, 77 ; on Shepherd of Hermas, 81.
Evangelical doctrines, 147.
Evolution and the Bible, 198.

Fairbairn, Professor Patrick, on quotations from the Old Testament in the New, 191, 193.
Fathers of the second century, value of their testimony concerning the canon, 71sq., 154.
Final cause of Old Testament history, 117sq.
Forgery, Second Peter not a, 79; unsuccessful attempts at, 81.

Genealogical tables, use of, 216.
Genealogy, of Christ, 120, 201 ; of Melchizedek, 122.
Genesis and geology, 195-200.
Geology and the Bible, 195-200.
Gesenius on the meaning of *Elohim*, 190.
Glacial period, date of, 203.
Gospels, application of the Old Testament prophecies in the, 117sq.
Grammars, use of, 133.
Greek, the, of the New Testament, 143 ; not spoken by Christ, 173.
Guyot, Professor Arnold, on Genesis and geology, 197 ; on evolution, 198.

Hagiographa, 46.
Harmony, of the Gospels, 183 ; of the Bible with science, chapter on, 195-203.
Hebrews, Epistle to the, testimony concerning its canonicity, 75sq.; relation of, to Paul, 82, 108 ; character of, 121sq.; quotations in from the Old Testament, 121sq., 189.
Hermeneutics, of the Rabbis, 108 ; of Paul, 108, 114 ; of the Book of Hebrews, 108 ; proper method of, 110sq.; of Christ, 112-114; formula for, 141.
Holy Spirit, special promise of the, to the apostles, 19sq.
Hort. See *Westcott*.
Humility necessary to an interpreter, 102, 205, 230.

Imprecatory Psalms, 213sq.
Incarnation, analogous to inspiration, 211.
Incomprehensibility of God, 124.

Induction, method of, 218 ; inspiration proved by, 219sq., 228sq.
Infallibility, sphere of, 14, 101, 149 ; not possessed by interpreters, 101, 148.
Inspiration, defined, 14, 101 ; promise of, 18sq., 152 ; claimed by the apostles, 26sq., 153 ; objections to Paul's claim of, 29sq., 211 ; of the Old Testament, 35sq.; of the Bible confirmed by its typical language, 123 ; argument for, 151-156 ; mode of, 157, 159sq.; doctrine of, analogous to that of design, 157sq., 204 ; produces variety and makes the Bible an organic whole, 209sq.; human elements in, 211 ; analogous to incarnation, 211 ; does not imply omniscience, 212; proved by induction, 219sq.; argument for, cumulative, 228.
Intelligibility of the Bible, 148.
Interpretation, biblical, 101 ; province of, 104 ; of illustrations, 208 ; of Job, 209 ; of Proverbs, 209 ; the true basis of doctrine, 232.
Interpretation of the Old Testament by Christ, 49, 110sq.; by Paul, 108, 114sq.; by the apostles, 110sq.; by the apostolic church, 122.
Interpretation of Scripture, chapter on, 101-150 ; rules of, 105sq.; of the obscure by the plain, 106 ; of Scripture by Scripture, 107, 126sq.
Irenæus, on Hebrews, 76 ; referred to Epistle of James, 77; on Second John, 78 ; on Revelation of John, 80 ; on Shepherd of Hermas, 81 ; quotes much from the New Testament, 86; on the New Testament, 154.

James, Epistle of, canonicity, 77, 82.
Jericho, blind men at, 134.
Jerome, on the canon of the Old Testament, 65 ; on the canon of the New, 71 ; on the Revelation of John, 80.
Jerusalem, destruction of, 125.
Jesus, son of Sirach, views of the Old Testament, 68.
Job, interpretation of, 209.
John, contemporaries of, 71 ; Second and Third Epistles of, canonicity of, 77 ; Revelation of, 79sq.
Jonah, story of, defended, 213.

236　　INDEX.

Josephus, on the Old Testament, 61sq.
Jude, Epistle of, canonicity, 77, 82.
Jude, relation of, to James, 77, 82.
Justin Martyr, 79, 86, 154.

Ladd, Rev. George T., his views on the canon criticised, 58; his views respecting the ability of the New Testament writers to interpret the Old, criticised, 108sq.; on alleged discrepancies, 175sq.; on alleged errors in quotation, 184.
Language, pregnant, 123; elasticity of, 132sq., 142, 171, 174, 196; can convey definite truth, 138, 146; changes in, 143; deterioration of, 144.
Lexicons, use of, 132, 133.
Lightfoot, his views of the word Scripture criticised, 41.
Luke represents Paul, 82.

Manuscripts of the New Testament enumerated, 87.
Mark represents Peter, 82.
Mediums, so-called, 164.
Melchizedek, type of Christ, 111, 122; genealogy of, omitted in Genesis, 122.
Melito, on the canon of the Old Testament, 64.
Miracles, an essential element of Christianity, 15sq.; power of performing, conferred on the apostles, 19; number of, performed by the apostles, 20; by Peter, 21; by Stephen, 22; by Philip, 22; by Paul, 23sq.; by Barnabas, 23; by the author of the Book of Hebrews, 24.
Mosaic code, humaneness of, 214.
Muratorian Canon, books contained in, 73sq.; did not contain Hebrews, 76; contains Jude, 77; did not contain Epistle of James, 77; on Revelation, 80; on Shepherd of Hermas, 81.

Nature, cruelty of, 216.
Nazareth, derivation of, 118.
Neptune, discovery of, 226.
New Testament, supernatural element of, 15sq.; apostolic authorship of, 82; language of, 143; character of, 154.
Noah began to be an husbandman, 185.

Old Testament, supernatural element of, 15sq.; inspiration of, asserted by the New, 35sq., 53,

153; asserted by the writers themselves, 50sq.; threefold division of, 46, 56sq.; books of, enumerated, 57; typical character of, 111sq.; relation of, to the New, 120, 123.
Origen, on the canon of the Old Testament, 65; on the Book of Hebrews, 76; on Jude, 77; on Second Peter, 78; on Revelation of John, 80; quotes Epistle of Barnabas, 81; quotes Shepherd of Hermas, 81; abounds in quotations from the New Testament,86.

Pantaenus on the Book of Hebrews, 75.
Parables, use of, 126.
Parallelisms between the Old Testament and the history of Christ, 118.
Passover, time of the last, 135sq.; elasticity of the word, 137.
Paul, miracles of, 23sq.; inspiration of, objected to, 29sq., 211; inspiration claimed by Peter for, 29sq.; thought to disclaim inspiration, 29sq.; his method of interpretation, 108, 114sq.; his quotations from the Old Testament, 115sq.; his anticipations of Christ's second coming, 126sq.
Perfection, relative character of, 101, 205.
Peter, miracles of, 21sq.; his wife's mother healed, 171.
Peter, Second, canonicity of, 78.
Philip, miracles of, 22.
Philo, his reverence for the Old Testament, 64; his neglect of the Apocrypha, 64.
Pilgrim's Progress compared with Esther, 210.
πνεῦμα, 111.
Presumptions favoring the doctrine of inspiration, 17, 73.
Priesthood of Christ, 112.
Proof, burden of, 131, 155, 183.
Prophecy, foreshortened view of, 125.
Protestantism, theology of, independent of the Apocrypha, 83; views respecting the Bible, 148.
Proverbs, Book of, interpretation of, 209.
Purgatory, doctrine of, inculcated by the Apocrypha, 67, 83.

Quenstedt, 161.
Quotations, from the Old Testament in the New, 34, 47, 111sq.; almost none from other books,

47; books of the Old Testament not quoted in the New, 55; formulas of, 117; difficult of explanation, 120; Alleged errors in, chapter on, 184-194.

Rabbins, hermeneutical method of, 108; partially endorsed by Paul, 117.
Resurrection of Christ, evidential value of, 16sq.
Revelation, manifold character of, 102; difficulties of a written, 104.
Revelation of John, claims divine authority, 32; its canonicity, 79.
Row, Rev. C. A., his views of inspiration criticised, 30sq.
Rudimentary organs, 204; ideal value of, 207.

Salem, 122.
Science, and the Bible, chapter on, 195-203; chronology of the Bible compared with that of, 200-203.
Scripture, use of the word, in the time of Christ, 37sq.; the singular means the same as the plural, 40sq.
Second century, testimony of the, to the canon, 71sq.; value of this testimony, 72, 153.
Second coming of Christ, Paul's anticipation of, 126sq.
Seed, difference in meaning of the singular and plural, 116.
Seeds, transportation of, 206.
Septuagint, 65.
Sermon on the Mount, 49sq., 181sq.
Sewall, Professor J. B., 214.
Shepherd of Hermas, not canonical, 75, 81.
Sinaitic manuscript contains Epistle of Barnabas and the Shepherd of Hermas, 81; age of, 87; value of, 94sq., 99.
Sodom and Gomorrah, destruction of, 216.
Solomon's Songs compared with Westminster Catechism, 210.
Spiritualists, doctrine of, 164.
Stuart, Professor Moses, on the inspiration of Paul, 29; on the Old Testament, 45sq.; on quotations in Hebrews, 192.
Supernatural, extent of the, in the Bible, 15sq., 152.
Syriac Version, books contained in, 73; contains Hebrews, 75; does not contain Jude, 77; contains James, 77; does not contain Revelation, 80.

Talmud, composition of, 47; on the canon of the Old Testament, 65.
Tempest, account of stilling of, 172.
Tertullian on Hebrews, 76; on Jude, 77; on the Shepherd of Hermas, 81; abounds in quotations from the New Testament, 86.
Tholuck, quoted, 117.
Tischendorf, discovers the Sinaitic manuscript, 87; his critical Greek Testament, 88.
Toy, Professor C. H., his view of Hebrews criticised, 108; his views of the inability of the New Testament writers to interpret the Old criticised, 108sq.; on New Testament quotations, 189sq.
Tradition, limits within which it is authoritative, 71sq., 154.
Translation, difficulty of, 188.
Translations. See *Versions.*
Tregelles, rank as a textual critic, 99.
Trent, council of, on the canon, 66sq.
Types of the Old Testament, 111sq., 121.

Unity of the Bible, 221.
Usher, Archbishop, chronology of, 201.

Variations in the text of the New Testament, number of, 88; mostly trivial, 88; the more important enumerated, 91sq.; origin of, 95sq.
Vatican manuscript, age of, 87; value of, 94, 99.
Versions of the Old Testament, Greek, 65; Syriac, 73, 75, 86; Latin, 73, 86; Egyptian, 86; English, 227.
Vulgate, endorsed by the Council of Trent, 68.

Waste in nature, 205.
Westminster Catechism compared with Solomon's Songs, 210.
Westcott and Hort, on the Greek text of the New Testament, 90.
Westcott's Epistles of St. John, 78.
Wharton, Rev. Francis, on words, 139sq.
Word, analogy between the written and the incarnate, 103.

Zarephath, Elijah at, 186.

INDEX OF SCRIPTURE PASSAGES.

	PAGE
Genesis i.	196
i. 1, 20, 21, 27	198
ii. 4	196
ix. 20, 21	185
x. 15-18	202
xii. 3	39
xv. 6	40
xv. 16	214
xxi. 10, 12	39
xxi. 10	114
Exodus iii. 5	103
iii. 6	36, 113
iv. 12	50
ix. 16	36
xii. 49	214
xxii. 21	214
xxiii. 9, 12	214
xxiii. 18	137
xxvi. 6	217
xxxiii. 19	36
xxxiv. 16	50
Leviticus xi. 5	165
xviii. 5	36
xix. 18	40
xxiv. 22	214
Numbers ix. 14	214
xv. 15, 16, 29	214
xvi. 28	50
xxxv. 15	214
Deuteronomy i. 16	214
ix. 1	196
x. 18, 19	214
xxv. 4	39, 115
xxvi. 12	214
xxxii. 21	36
xxxii. 43	189
1 Samuel xxiv., xxvi.	214
2 Samuel xxii. 3	121
xxiii. 2	51
1 Chronicles iii. 11, 12	201
vi. 7-11	201
xxvi. 24	202

	PAGE
2 Chronicles xxx. 18, 22	137
1 Kings xvii. 1	186
xvii. 9 ff.	185
xviii. 1	186
xix. 10, 14	39
xix. 18	36
xxi. 2	134
Ezra ix. 1-4	51
Nehemiah viii. 1	51
Job xx. 15	121
Psalms viii	190
viii. 5	121
xvi. 10	116
xl. 6-8	192
xlv. 6, 7	122
lxxxii. 6	190
xcv. 11	122
xcvi. 5	121
xcvii. 7	121, 189
cii. 25-27	121
cx.	36, 111, 112
cx. 1	122
cx. 4	111, 122
cxviii.	38
cxviii. 22	40
cxviii. 27	137
cxix.	63
cxxxviii. 1	121
Ecclesiastes iv. 4	40
Proverbs xxi. 31	120
Isaiah i. 2	51
i. 3	42
iv. 2	118
vii. 14-16	119
viii. 17, 18	121
xi. 1	118
xxviii. 16	40
xxix. 13	187
xxix. 18	112
xxxv. 8	102
liii. 7	39

INDEX OF SCRIPTURE PASSAGES. 239

Isaiah liii. 12	112
liv. 1	114
lviii. 6	112
lxi. 1, 2	112
Jeremiah i. 4	51
xvii. 25	120
xxiii. 5	118
Daniel ix. 26, 27	113
ix. 27	112
xi. 31	112
xii. 11	112
Hosea xi. 1	118
xiv. 3	120
Zechariah iii. 8	118
vi. 12	118
ix. 9	120
xiii. 7	112
Malachi ii. 3	137
iii. 1	97
Matthew i. 1-17	201
i. 22, 23	119
i. 22	117
ii. 15	117
ii. 23	118
iii. 17	98
iv. 14	117
iv. 24	167
v.-vii.	181
v. 22	92
viii. 15	171
viii. 25	172
viii. 29	167
viii. 31	168
viii. 33	96
x. 1	19
x. 8	168
x. 9, 10	178
x. 19, 20	19
xi. 10	97
xi. 13	46
xii. 24-32	168
xii. 43 sq.	168
xiii. 13	124
xiii. 14	36
xiii. 31, 32	165
xiii. 55	77
xv. 4	35
xv. 9	187
xvi., xxiv.	125
xvi. 28	127
xviii. 20	95
xviii. 28	96
xix. 7	176
xix. 17	175
xx. 29-34	134
xxi. 4	117

Matthew xxi. 42	38, 43
xxii. 29	43
xxii. 31	36
xxii. 32	113
xxii. 40	46
xxii. 43	36, 111
xxiii. 35	57
xxiv.	130
xxiv. 15	112
xxiv. 34	127
xxiv. 36	110
xxiv. 37 sq.	184
xxv. 6	95
xxvi. 2	137
xxvi. 17-30	136
xxvi. 18, 19	137
xxvi. 24, 54, 56	113
xxvi. 31	112
xxvi. 54	43
xxvi. 56	43, 44
xxvii. 37	177
Mark i. 2	97
i. 11	98
i. 24, 25	167
i. 31	171
i. 32	167
iii. 22-30	168
iv. 31	165
iv. 38	172
v. 7	167
v. 12	168
vi. 8, 9	178
vii. 10	36
ix. 13	113
ix. 28, 29	168
x. 3	176
x. 18	175
x. 46-52	134
xii. 10, 11	38
xii. 26	36
xii. 36	36, 111
xiii. 11	19
xiv. 12-26	136
xiv. 12	137
xiv. 49	117
xv. 26	177
xvi. 10-20	92, 93
Luke i. 51-55	35
iv. 18, 19	112
iv. 21	41
iv. 25-27	185
iv. 39	171
iv. 41	167
vi. 17-49	181
vi. 17, 18	167
vii. 27	97
viii. 24	172
viii. 32	168
viii. 34	96
ix. 1	19

240 INDEX OF SCRIPTURE PASSAGES.

Luke ix. 3	178
x. 7	39
x. 17-20	168
x. 17	20
x. 18 sq.	168
xi. 15-23	168
xii. 11, 12	19
xvi. 16	46
xvi. 29, 31	46
xvi. 31	45
xviii. 19	175
xviii. 35-43	134
xix. 1	134
xx. 17	38
xx. 37	36
xx. 42	36, 111
xxi. 14, 15	19
xxii. 1-20	136
xxii. 1	137
xxii. 7	137
xxii. 8, 13	137
xxii. 37	112
xxiii. 38	177
xxiv. 27, 44, 45	43
xxiv. 27, 44	56, 113
xxiv. 27	46
xxiv. 44	46
xxiv. 53	96
John i. 14	79
i. 45	46
i. 46	118
ii. 13	137
ii. 19	124
ii. 22	42
iii. 14	113
iv., vi.	115
v. 1	141
v. 4	92, 137
v. 39, 46	113
v. 39	43
vi. 4	137
vii. 38, 42	42
vii. 38	113
vii. 40-43	38
viii. 1-11	93
ix. 2	119
x.	112
x. 35	38, 42, 190
xi. 50	123
xii. 15	120
xii. 32	124
xii. 38	117
xii. 39	36
xiii.-xvii.	179
xiii. 1	135
xiii. 18	113, 117
xiv.-xvi.	19
xiv. 26	19
xv. 26, 27	20
xvi. 12-15	20
xvii. 12	113

John xviii. 28	135, 137
xix. 14, 31	135
xix. 20	177
xix. 24, 28, 36, 37	38, 117
xix. 28	42
xix. 35	79
xix. 37	41
xx. 9	38
xx. 30, 31	174
xxi. 22	127
Acts i. 16	38
ii. 34, 35	111
ii. 43	21
iii. 1-10	21
v. 1-11	21
v. 12-16	21
vi. 8	22
viii. 5-8, 13	23
viii. 32	42
viii. 35	39
ix. 33-35	22
ix. 36-41	22
ix. 42	22
xiii. 11	23
xiii. 15	46
xiii. 35	116
xiv. 3	23
xiv. 10	23
xv. 13	77
xv. 28	26
xvi. 16 sq.	165
xvi. 18	24
xvii. 11	44
xvii. 28	48
xviii. 24, 28	44
xx. 10, 12	24
xxiv. 14	46
xxviii. 1-6	24
xxviii. 9	24
xxviii. 23	46
xxviii. 25	36
Romans i. 1	27, 88
i. 2	44
i. 3	89
i. 4	89
i. 7	89, 90
i. 8	90
iii. 5	29
iii. 21	46
iv.	108
iv. 3	39, 42
iv. 11, 17	116
vi. 19	29
ix. 8, 9, 13, 15, 17, 25, 29, 33	116
ix. 15	36
ix. 17	36, 39, 42
x. 5	36
x. 11	39, 42
x. 19	36
xi. 2	39, 42

INDEX OF SCRIPTURE PASSAGES.

Romans xi. 4	36
xv. 4	44
xv. 10	37
xv. 18, 19	25
xvi. 26	44
1 Corinthians i. 1	27
i. 14–17	212
v. 7	137
vii. 6	29
vii. 12	30
vii. 25	30
vii. 40	30
ix. 1, 2	27
ix. 9, 10	115
x. 1–4	115
xiii.	144
xiv. 37	28
xv. 3, 4	44
xv. 9	27
xv. 51	127
2 Corinthians i. 1	27
vi. 16	37
xi., xii.	30
xi. 5	27
xi. 17	31
xii. 11, 12	25, 27, 31
Galatians i. 1	27
i. 11, 12	28
iii.	108
iii. 8, 22	39, 42
iii. 8	39, 116
iii. 15	29
iii. 16	115
iii. 23	41
iv.	108
iv. 21–31	114
iv. 27	114, 116
iv. 30	30, 42, 114
Ephesians i. 1	27
ii. 20	27
Philippians iv. 5	127
Colossians i. 1	27
1 Thessalonians ii. 13	27
iv. 15, 17	126
2 Thessalonians ii. 2, 3	129
1 Timothy i. 1	27
i. 4	92
ii. 7	27
iii. 16	92
v. 18	39, 42, 115
1 Timothy v. 23	211
2 Timothy i. 1, 11	27
iii. 14–17	33, 34
iii. 16	39, 41
iv. 13	211
Titus i. 1	27
i. 12	48
Hebrews i. 1	104, 159
i. 6–8	37
i. 6	121, 189
i. 8, 9	121
i. 10–12	121
i. 13	36, 111, 122
ii. 3, 4	25, 28
ii. 7	121
ii. 12	37
ii. 13	121
iii. 7	37
iv. 3–5, 9, 10	122
iv. 3, 4	37
v. 6	37
vii. 2, 3	122
vii. 17	122
x. 5, 15	37
x. 5–10	191
x. 34	91
xi. 9, 10, 13–16	122
xi. 28	137
xii. 26	37
xiii. 5	37
James ii. 8, 23	40
iv. 5	40
1 Peter ii. 6	40, 42
iv. 7	127
2 Peter i. 1	79
i. 20	40, 42
iii. 1	79
iii. 2	28
iii. 8	129
iii. 15, 16	29
iii. 16	44
1 John i. 1	18
i. 2	79
iv. 1	169
v. 7, 8	93
Jude 14	47
Revelation i. 1–9	79
i. 10, 11	32
xxii. 8, 9	79
xxii. 18, 19	32

A BOOK FOR THE TIMES.

AN INQUIRY CONCERNING
THE
Relation of Death to Probation.

Written for the Congregational Publishing Society by

PROF. G. FREDERICK WRIGHT,
AUTHOR OF "THE LOGIC OF CHRISTIAN EVIDENCES," AND "STUDIES IN SCIENCE AND RELIGION."

Post-paid, 75 cents.

"If you like a book which takes hold of its subject with a grip and handles it fairly and handsomely, and at the same time positively and thoroughly, you have it here. Few men are entitled to speak with so much weight on the point as Professor Wright. He is a confessed expert, a scientist in high standing. We commend the volume heartily to our readers, whatever their present opinions upon its subject." — *Congregationalist.*

"We highly commend it for its faithful and clear presentation of the Scriptural teaching on this subject. Of course, this would be that there is no warrant in Scripture for believing that there is probation after death, but that the awards of the Judgment Day are endless." — *National Baptist, Phila.*

"This is a very clear, Scriptural, satisfactory discussion of a difficult subject. It is an especial tract for the hour, and should be widely circulated." — *Zion's Herald.*

"This book is serviceable as a fair, simple, and earnest statement of the usual doctrine of Future Punishment." — *Literary World.*

"The position of the author is highly conservative, especially in the discussion of proof-texts, and he contends for the received opinion that probation ends with death with a keen, practical appreciation of the homiletic importance of that doctrine." — *Independent, New York.*

"It discusses the questions that have been suggested in regard to a possible probation between death and the judgment, especially for those who have not had the motives of the gospel presented to them in this life. In it the reader will find the Scriptural aspect of the subject of eternal punishment presented so briefly, so clearly, so conclusively, that to avoid the issue he must make some compromise with his faith in the Word of God." — *Observer, New York.*

For Sale by all Booksellers, or sent, post-paid, on receipt of price, by

Congregational Publishing Society, Boston.

GEO. P. SMITH, Agent.

CHRIST PREACHING TO SPIRITS IN PRISON.

BY REV. WILLIAM DE LOSS LOVE.

Postpaid, 90 cents.

"We heartily commend the volume as an able, somewhat original, and thoroughly candid discussion. The author's treatment of the former passage is especially skilful, and the ability with which he has presented his views will be recognized by all who have given the subject close attention. The book is brief, but comprehensive. It is one of the most useful which the recent discussions of its subject have called out, and it deserves careful study." — *Congregationalist.*

"The essay is valuable for its scope in gathering the literature of the subject, as well as for its special theory of interpreting this somewhat difficult Scripture." — *Zion's Herald.*

"The work has the indorsement of Professor Tyler, of Amherst, for strength of material and originality of method — an opinion in which the public will fully concur." — *Advance.*

"His argument is written with his characteristic fidelity and painstaking study, making it worthy of a most careful perusal." — *Sunday-school World.*

"We recommend this book to any who are in doubt on this important subject. Not only has the author demonstrated that it is not necessary to write a folio volume in order to show broad scholarship, but, far more important, he has proved that the oracles of God yield their true meaning to patient and devout study." — *Northampton Gazette and Courier.*

"It is an able discussion of the knotty and long-debated question, with fresh views upon collateral points in eschatology." — *Illustrated Christian Weekly.*

"The argument is supported with much learning, and shows great research and study. It is altogether the most rational and scripturally truthful presentation of the subject yet made." — *Holyoke Transcript.*

"We have found it to be learned, ingenious, and interesting." — *Christian Advocate.*

"It displays careful research and comparison among the authorities." — *Springfield Republican.*

CONGREGATIONAL SUNDAY-SCHOOL AND PUBLISHING SOCIETY.

SABBATH ESSAYS.

A

WORK OF PERMANENT VALUE ON A THEME OF VITAL IMPORTANCE.

Price, $1.50.

As a treatise on the Sabbath, designed to meet all ordinary inquiries on the subject, it will be *invaluable to Pastors, Sabbath-School Teachers, Public and Private Libraries.* It is the most valuable contribution recently made to the literature on the Sabbath question.

The book contains thirty-eight essays and addresses, discussing the Sabbath in thirty-eight different aspects and relations. The essays are divided into sections, as follows: "The Sabbath in Nature," "The Sabbath in the Word of God," "The Sabbath in History," "The Sabbath in the State and in Society." The addresses follow, twelve in number, most of them on practical questions of Sabbath observance. A Historical Sketch on Sabbath Conventions closes the volume. The views of some of the foremost men of all the evangelical denominations are here brought together, presenting this great subject on all sides, furnishing a discussion that seems complete, and making the volume an invaluable text-book on the Sabbath question.

For Sale by all Booksellers, or sent, post-paid, on receipt of price, by

Congregational Publishing Society, Boston.

GEO. P. SMITH, Agent.

www.ingramcontent.com/pod-product-compliance
Lightning Source LLC
Chambersburg PA
CBHW031743230426
43669CB00007B/454